Robert Half On
HIRING ━━━

Books by Robert Half

The Robert Half Way to Get Hired in Today's Job Market
Robert Half's Success Guide for Accountants
Robert Half On Hiring

Robert Half On
HIRING—

by
ROBERT HALF

CROWN PUBLISHERS, INC.
NEW YORK

Published by Crown Publishers, Inc., One Park Avenue, New York, New York 10016 and simultaneously in Canada by General Publishing Company Limited.
Manufactured in the United States of America

Library of Congress Cataloging in Publication Data
Half, Robert.
    Robert Half on hiring.

    Includes index.
    1. Recruiting of employees. I. Title.
HF5549.5.R44H26   1985   658.3'11   84–16957
ISBN 0-517-55436-4

10 9 8 7 6 5 4 3 2

To Maxine,
who "hired" me
as her husband
forty years ago

CONTENTS

ACKNOWLEDGMENTS

Someone who gets no help makes no progress.

I had a great deal of help from many people, including company clients that had dealt with franchised offices of Robert Half International Inc., the managers of these offices, and thousands of candidates for employment, whose comments about finding jobs and employment interviews assisted me in developing hiring techniques. And Burke Marketing Research, a company that implemented studies that I have conceived to take the guesswork out of some employment concepts.

And there are nine people who were extremely helpful: Kenneth Asch, A. Bernard Frechtman, Alvin Galland, Marc Silbert, Barry Tarshis, Sanford Teller, James W. Thomas, Jane von Mehren, and James O. Wade.

INTRODUCTION

*People who hire the most often
know the least about hiring.*

No management function is more critical than the hiring of people who will go on to become competent, motivated, and productive employees. That's why it is both ironic and surprising that the vast majority of hiring decisions for key jobs in business are made by people who are essentially novices at the game—people, that is, who lack the experience and the skills needed to make hiring decisions on the basis of something other than how they happen to "feel" about a particular candidate after one or two interviews.

This is not opinion, but fact. It's a fact, too, that most hiring decisions are made by people who rarely hire more than one or two employees a year. It's a fact that most organizations and businesses are too small to afford a personnel professional. And it's a fact that even in large corporations, according to a survey by Burke Marketing Research commissioned expressly for this book, roughly 90 percent of the hiring for jobs that pay more than $40,000 is done by management and not by the personnel department.

The situation I describe would not be a problem if the hiring procedures of most companies today were effective. But such is not the case. It's no secret that each year American companies spend an astronomical amount of time, money, and energy on newly hired employees who either quit or are eventually terminated. And a recent study by the U.S. Labor Department shows that only about 50 percent of newly hired employees last more than six months in the job for which they were hired. True, some of the employees in this group are promoted or transferred, but it's safe to assume that the majority of those 50 percent simply don't work out and either leave on their own or are fired.

But the problem of ineffective hiring goes beyond the disturbingly high proportion of employees who either quit or are terminated within a few months after being hired. It extends to the millions of employees who, while they don't quit and aren't terminated, never make a *meaningful* contribution to their companies. I think of them as "phantom" employees: they show up for work every day, but considering what they accomplish, you would never guess they were on the payroll.

Then again, I don't want to paint too bleak a picture. Based on my experience, I am convinced that the vast majority of hiring mistakes being made today can be prevented. That is why I have written this book.

My purpose can be explained very simply. I want to

improve your ability to make intelligent hiring decisions and to help you choose the people best suited for the jobs it is your responsibility to fill.

I hope to do this is in two ways.

First, I want to broaden your understanding of the *hiring process* and help you better appreciate the logic that underlies a successful approach to the process.

Second, I want to share with you specific concepts and techniques that you will be able to apply to your own hiring situations and thereby enhance your chances of choosing the best person possible for each job you need to fill.

This is *not* a book on personnel theory. I have focused instead on the methods that are the most practical concern to managers, supervisors, and professionals who want to improve their ability to recruit and hire the best people.

You'll learn, for example, the best ways of putting together a job description that does more than simply *describe* a job but identifies the qualifications and attributes necessary to handle the job successfully.

You'll learn the best ways to increase the number of qualified applicants through effective recruiting procedures.

You'll learn the best ways to screen the candidates you recruit, and how to narrow the field without eliminating candidates who merit consideration.

You'll learn the best ways to prepare for and conduct an employment interview: what questions to ask and what interpretations to draw from the answers.

You'll learn the best ways to go about getting useful reference information.

You'll learn specific—and original—techniques that will help you bring as much objectivity as possible to the ultimate hiring decision.

You'll learn how to avoid the growing number of discriminatory actions now being brought against companies that, in many cases, were not even *aware* they were discriminating.

Finally, you'll learn specific steps to take *after* you've made the decision, so that you make sure you land the candidate of your choice.

What you *won't* find in this book are sure-fire formulas for hiring the right person—and for a good reason: there *are* no such formulas. Because hiring is ultimately a matter of predicting human behavior, it is not a science. Hiring is an art. So, for every principle we discuss in this book, there will be exceptions: "can't miss" candidates who turn out to be major hiring mistakes, and "clearly unqualified" candidates who turn out to be superstars.

To illustrate my point, let me tell you about an experience we had years ago in our New York office in which a candidate who showed up for an interview by mistake ended up with the job. What happened, briefly, was that a client had asked us to arrange interviews in our office for four candidates out of six whose résumés we'd submitted. One of the candidates, as it happened, had a very common name, and one of our new placement managers inadvertently called up a *different* man with the same name and asked him to come to the office on the morning of the interview.

We recognized our mistake, of course, as soon as the wrong candidate showed up at the office, and we also recognized that this candidate didn't have the specific background the client was looking for. But even after we explained all of this, the client decided that he'd interview the candidate anyway, in addition to the three others. In the end the client decided that the candidate who'd showed up by mistake was the best person for the job.

On the surface, it may seem illogical that someone who not only lacked the specific background for the position but, by all rights, shouldn't have been interviewed in the first place would be hired for this position. In this particular instance, however, the decision *was* logical. True, the candidate didn't have the *specific* background the client was looking for, but he had skills and attributes that gave him the edge over the other contenders. The logic, in other words, was *there*. It simply wasn't apparent from the résumé.

If there is a single message to this book, it lies in this very point: the fact that while the logic behind the best hiring decision may not be apparent, there is nonetheless a logical way—specific steps you can take at each stage in the hiring process—to greatly enhance your chances of choosing the best person for each job you have to fill.

1 | *THE HIRING PROCESS*

*It's easy to make good decisions
when there are no bad options.*

A successful retailing executive I know was recently bemoaning the fact that he was in a hiring "slump." It seems that the last three or four people he had hired in his department had lasted only a few months on the job, and the executive couldn't figure out why. "The really frustrating part," he was saying, "is that I've always prided myself on being a great judge of character."

I mention this executive at this early stage of the book for a very specific reason: namely, that his basic perception about hiring—that hiring successfully is primarily a matter of "judging character"—is typical of the perceptions most people have of hiring, and it goes a long way to explain why so many hiring decisions end so badly.

Don't misunderstand. I'm not minimizing the value of being able to judge people when it comes to making good hiring decisions. To the contrary, much of the skill at the root of successful hiring is embodied in your ability to make character judgments relatively quickly, and often on the basis of sketchy evidence. The point, though, is that the "judging" aspect of hiring is only *one* of the tools of an effective hiring strategy.

Think about it a moment. It's possible that you, too, like the executive I just mentioned, have made hiring choices you later came to regret, and that when this happened you also questioned your "judgment." Like most people, you probably interviewed several candidates, asked what you felt were relevant questions, and then made what you felt at the time was the most intelligent decision.

Has it ever occurred to you that your ultimate decision did not take into consideration all of the important facts? Consider some of these other possibilities:

• Maybe you didn't analyze the job properly before you started to look, and, as a result, didn't attract the kind of candidates necessary for the particular job that needed to be filled.

• You may not have used your recruiting sources wisely enough, and thus cut down on the number of qualified candidates you had to choose from.

• You may have inadvertently eliminated from consideration (on the basis of a résumé, perhaps) someone who could have done the job far better than the person you ultimately hired.

- You may have failed during the interviews to secure enough relevant information on which to make a rational, intelligent decision.

- You may not have been diligent enough about checking references (if, in fact, you even bothered to check references).

I could list some other possibilities, but by now you should see what I'm getting at. Hiring is *not* simply a matter of interviewing a number of candidates and deciding which of them is the best qualified. Hiring is a complex process, of which interviewing candidates is only one aspect.

It could be argued, I suppose, that because most hiring decisions involve an interview at some point along the way, interviewing candidates is the single most important aspect of the process. This may well be true, but the importance of interviewing should not diminish the importance of all the other elements that go into successful hiring. Analyzing the job requirements, using the best recruiting sources, screening effectively, preparing properly for the interview, being diligent in your reference checking—these are critical considerations too. And when there are breakdowns in any of these elements, the entire process is compromised.

It's worth stressing, too, that some of the factors that affect hiring decisions have nothing to do with hiring per

3

se, but may have more to do with you, with your department, or with the kind of company you run. I know of several companies whose personnel reputations are so bad that only very desperate candidates would ever apply there, which means that it's almost impossible, practically speaking, for these companies to make a "good" hiring choice. By the same token, I know of other companies whose reputations are such that they can almost always attract quality candidates.

I don't mean to dwell too much on what may seem to you to be an obvious point—simply to underscore the importance as you read through this book of appreciating the *totality* of the hiring process, and of appreciating, above all, how the various elements in hiring relate to one another. Ideally, in fact, if you follow an intelligent route throughout the process, you dramatically minimize the possibility of making a "wrong" choice when it comes to making the final decision—it's more a matter of being "less right."

Some Observations on the Legal Aspects of Hiring

It is impossible to discuss hiring today without touching upon the legal issues that have arisen over the past three decades as a consequence of the growing number of federal and state laws against discrimination in employment. Company personnel directors and managers, of course, are familiar with these laws and sensitive to their requirements, but businesspeople who hire are frequently unaware of how tough these regulations are and how easy it is to inadvertently violate these laws.

I will be looking into the legal ramifications of most of the areas covered in this book, and I am indebted in this regard to A. Bernard Frechtman, a member of the law firm of Pollner, Mezan, Stolzberg and Frechtman, and one of the country's foremost authorities on employment law.

As Mr. Frechtman points out, most managers responsible for hiring today are generally aware of the broad areas in which discrimination is prohibited—race, religion, national origin, age, sex, marital status, and handicap—but few truly understand the subtlety of some of their own activities or the language that can constitute such discrimination.

On the other hand, one doesn't have to be a lawyer to avoid trouble. Says Mr. Frechtman: "You don't need a great deal of information. You simply need to be familiar with certain laws, and you need to approach each hiring situation with your mind set on the concept of equality."

The long and short of the federal and state laws and regulations that have been passed in recent years with respect to job discrimination is twofold.

First of all, the hiring standards you use must be *job-*

5

related (as opposed to person-related) and, in particular, must be related to job *performance*. If you establish a specific hiring standard (for example, that the employee must be a certain weight or height and if this requirement disproportionately eliminates a particular group of people), you are required to prove that this standard is indeed *necessary* to job performance.

The same principle holds true for whatever individual criteria you establish as the basis of your hiring decision; these, too, must relate to job performance. If you use any sort of test to determine the suitability of a candidate for the job, for instance, you should be prepared to prove a *direct* correlation between the results of that test and the effectiveness of job performance.

Second, the standards you set for any job cannot adversely affect the hiring chances of any one group of people. In other words, no standard you set can lessen the chances of hiring of any group of people on the basis of race, religion, national origin, age, sex, marital status, or physical handicaps. And should a person who isn't hired have reason to *believe* that you took any of these factors into consideration, your company could find itself the target of a discrimination investigation or lawsuit.

There's more. If the job itself or the job environment is structured so that certain groups are not given an equal chance to perform the job effectively, this could be considered discriminatory, too. For example, you cannot deny women a job simply because your company has no physical facilities (rest rooms, for instance) for women. Nor can you deny a woman a job because the job might oblige her to travel with men. To the contrary, companies whose policies and procedures have historically denied opportunity to specific groups are now under pressure from the government to take steps (that is to say, affirmative action) to reverse these patterns.

Let me stress here that whether you or somebody else in your company is *deliberately* discriminating in any aspect of your hiring procedures is not an issue. It's no defense to say you didn't know it was discriminatory to ask a newly married woman if she intended to have children soon, or that it was discriminatory to ask a candidate where his or her parents were born. Such questions are simply illegal, and, so far as the officials responsible for enforcing discrimination legislation are concerned, it makes no difference whether the discrimination is the result of ignorance or of prejudicial design.

As it happens, there are certain exceptions to these laws. These exceptions are known as "bona fide occupational qualifications" (BFOQ), and they are set forth in Title VII of the Civil Rights Act and in state laws against job discrimination. The problem, though, is that it is rare that a job will require that a person be—or not be—of a certain religion, sex, or age. Bernard Frechtman's advice on the issue of bona fide occupational qualifications is quite clear: "Don't even *think* about exceptions, but approach each employment situation as if there *were* no exceptions."

| 2 | ON DECIDING WHAT YOU NEED |

Credentials are not the same as accomplishments.

The majority of hiring mistakes made each day could be prevented if the people responsible for the hiring simply did a more effective job of determining exactly what they were looking for *before* they started to look.

On the surface, deciding what you need in an employee seems simple enough. You just list the specific functions and responsibilities of the job and then determine the skills and attributes necessary to carry them out successfully. The problem, though, is that neither of these steps is as open-and-shut as it seems.

When you're listing functions and responsibilities, for instance, you can't automatically assume that what you are listing represents your genuine needs—not unless you've analyzed the job with great care and have been honest and realistic in your assessment. One of the complaints you hear over and over again from personnel directors in major corporations is that the job descriptions drawn up by the managers in their companies do not accurately reflect what the job truly requires. Key functions are sometimes omitted entirely or made to seem inconsequential, while minor functions are overemphasized.

And even if you've drawn up a description that accurately reflects a particular job, it's much more difficult than many people think to determine what specific qualifications are needed to handle that job successfully.

All of which explains why it is so essential that you yourself take the responsibility for drawing up the job description and for determining the criteria on which the hiring decision is to be based. Yes, you can seek all the input you want—from the personnel department, from colleagues, and from the departing employee. In the end, you will have to "live" with the person you hire, and you're the person who should be establishing these fundamental criteria.

Be particularly careful about the input you receive from the person leaving the job, even though he or she theoretically should know the needs of the job better than anybody else. The problem here is the natural tendency of people leaving a position to exaggerate the difficulty of their job. Sometimes this is done out of vanity, but sometimes employees exaggerate the qualifications so that you won't be able to find a replacement that quickly, thus leaving the door open in the event they want to come back to their old job. I've even heard of some cases in which departing employees who were asked to do the actual hiring (a big mistake, in my view) deliberately chose an incompetent replacement, not necessarily because they wanted to be missed, but because they wanted to be appreciated in their absence.

In any case, the very existence of a job vacancy gives you an unusual opportunity: a chance to reflect on your overall needs and perhaps to make changes in the job that might not have been possible with the employee who held the job previously. For better or worse, jobs have a tendency to assume the personality of the person holding them. And it's possible that you made certain compromises to accommodate the previous employee: reduced the amount of detail, perhaps, or made changes in the reporting hierarchy.

Writing Out the Job Description

The first thing to do when you're establishing hiring criteria is to write out a job description that does more than simply list specific duties and responsibilities of the job, but also indicates the relative importance of each duty and each responsibility.

There are different ways of going about it. Here's a procedure that's both simple and effective.

First, list all the duties and responsibilities the job re-

11

quires. Don't worry for now about the order, but try to be as specific as you can. Rather than simply writing "responsible for training," indicate the *kind* of training for which the employee will be responsible. Rather than then writing "administrative duties," list the *specific* tasks that need to be performed.

Once you've completed your list, go through it again and group each function listed into one of three categories: very important, important, not so important.

Once you've completed this grouping, you're ready to answer three questions:

1. Do you need somebody *new* to handle this job?
2. Is the job, as you've described it, doable?
3. What sort of an employee can you *expect* to hire?

Let's consider each question.

1. Do you need somebody new to handle the job?

Don't be too quick to answer this question.

Give thought to the possibility that the functions you've spelled out (particularly those that fall in the "very important" category) might be efficiently incorporated into a job already being filled by any of several good people on your staff.

You might also want to consider restructuring the job so that the lower-level functions are assigned to a new employee at a lower salary, and higher-level functions are assigned to somebody currently on your staff.

Such changes may not be appropriate in every situation, but consider *all* alternatives that might enhance the efficiency of your department, your company, or you.

2. Is the job doable?

If you're satisfied that you do need a new employee, look over your list of functions again and ask yourself if the job is truly *doable* as you've structured it.

Here, again, don't be in too much of a hurry to answer "yes." Don't assume that because you, or somebody else, was able to do the job, that this will hold true for other people as well.

Be particularly sensitive to responsibilities that might conflict with one another. One of our offices recently received a job description from an electronics manufacturer in need of a controller. The company wanted someone who would be responsible for doing detailed analysis, including economic projections and financial statements, and also wanted the candidate to be involved with customer relations.

I'm not saying that the company may not have had a *need* for such a person, only that it's not easy to find an accountant—or any specialist, for that matter—who is extremely detail-oriented and skilled at human relations as well.

13

Recognize the limitations you place on yourself when you establish job functions that aren't compatible. Bear in mind that people you supervised who handled incompatible functions may not have had this ability when you first hired them, but may have acquired it through on-the-job experience.

Review with scrupulous care each of the duties and responsibilities you've listed. See if you can picture somebody actually performing those functions. If you have doubts, here's a good test: estimate the number of hours per week the person who fills the job will have to spend on each function you've listed, and then add up the total hours. I did this once with a client who found that, by his own calculations, the person he hired would have to work seventy-seven hours a week.

You could find similarly distressing news about the list you've drawn up. But better to discover these problems now than later.

3. Whom can you expect to hire?

Years ago, I was approached by a mid-size company that was looking for a financial vice-president and wasn't in the mood to compromise. The person they wanted to hire, I was told, had to have an MBA from an Ivy League school and had to be currently holding the number one or number two position at a rival company. One more thing: the company didn't want to "give away the store" in order to lure this candidate.

As it happens, this company was on shaky ground at the time. As I tried to explain to the company president, an acquaintance of mine, why would a candidate who met these qualifications (assuming such a candidate existed) be interested in taking such a job? To paraphrase the familiar Groucho Marx line, anybody who could meet these qualifications and was still interested in the job was, by definition, somebody the company probably wouldn't want to hire.

The pattern is familiar. I call it the "superstar syndrome": setting the job qualifications so unrealistically high that you make it all but impossible to find a "qualified" candidate.

Mind you, I'm not arguing against establishing high standards. I'm simply cautioning you against confusing what you'd ideally *like* to have with what the reality of your situation *allows* you to have. You need to be brutally frank with yourself when you are establishing job criteria. You need to recognize that the job you're offering, as it's structured, may not be all that attractive to good candidates. You need to keep in mind that what you and others in your company may think of as an "exciting" business or a "challenging" opportunity may not seem exciting or challenging to most candidates. You need to take a hard look at your company's reputation—at its turnover rate, its status in the industry.

In addition, you need to take into consideration specific aspects of the job that candidates will be evaluating: How convenient or inconvenient is the *location* of your company? How attractive is the office environment? You have to compare the salary and the opportunities in your company with those being offered by competitive firms. In other words, you have to put yourself in the shoes of the good candidates you're going to be interviewing and think for a moment about what *they* are looking for.

Going through this little exercise could be instructive for you. You may discover, for instance, that to attract quality candidates you have to offer more money than competitive companies are paying for a comparable position. Or you may discover the need to sweeten the benefits somewhat.

There is nothing to be gained by *concealing* major negatives from candidates. Doing so is shortsighted and will almost always produce a hiring mistake—someone who will almost certainly leave once the truth is known.

Determining Hiring Criteria

The specific procedure I recommend for establishing hiring criteria is keyed to the H-I-R-E form on pages 168–169, which many clients of Robert Half International Inc. franchisees have been using successfully for many years.

You'll notice that the qualifications column has five categories:

16

1. Experience
2. Education
3. Intelligence
4. Appearance and personality
5. Other

You'll notice, too, that the form relies heavily on two additional factors: your impression of the candidate's innate ability to do the job and the candidate's motivation—his or her eagerness to do the job.

The logic behind the procedure I'm recommending is to take each aspect of the job and consider it in relation to the criteria on the form. For each specific task (particularly those in the "very important" category) you need to ask yourself the following questions:

• What sort of experience is *truly* necessary to perform each specific function?

• How much education is necessary?

• How intelligent must the person be to perform that function?

• How important is personal appearance to that function?

• What specific personality factors are necessary?

The chief value of establishing criteria in this way is that

17

it helps you to be reasonably objective. It forces you to look at the individual requirements of the job and then to base your overall perspective of the job on the sum of these requirements.

The procedure also gives you a natural way to establish priorities, and helps to prevent (although not necessarily eliminating) the tendency we all have to give more importance to attributes that we value but that may not have a bearing on job performance.

Keep in mind, however, that the criteria you eventually come up with are simply tools used for comparitive purposes, and not a formula for selection; we'll look into how you actually use this tool in making a selection later in the book. For now, let's examine some of the pitfalls that may await you when you are analyzing your needs with the H-I-R-E form.

Avoiding the Specifications Trap

Most jobs beyond entry level require a certain set of skills or experience or educational background. Whatever these requirements may be, they should be part of your job criteria.

If you're looking for a product designer, you need someone with a proven record of designing products similar to yours. If you need a standard cost accountant, you need someone with a standard cost accounting background. If you need an architect, you need someone who has acquired the appropriate degrees and licenses. These are your "mandatories."

There is a point, however, at which mandatories begin to work against you. Yes, in some situations—when you have more qualified candidates than you can possibly handle—arbitrary criteria serve a useful (if perhaps unfair) purpose. Generally, though, the more arbitrary your criteria, the fewer candidates you attract and the more you *lessen* your chances of finding the best person. One of the most successful hiring specialists I know has a simple rule she follows whenever she is listing mandatories: she uses a 3 × 5 index card and limits herself to only those mandatories that can fit on the card. Her explanation: whenever the mandatories you establish can't be limited to a 3 × 5 index card, you're probably being too restrictive.

There's another reason—more subtle, perhaps, but no less important—for limiting mandatories. It has to do with the priorities you establish when the time comes to evaluate the candidates you interview. Every study on employee turnover I've ever seen has produced essentially this same general finding: when people don't work out in jobs, it is rarely because they lack the *technical* skills or specific credentials; it's because of other considerations: a lack of motivation or the inability to blend into the work environment.

Think about yourself for a moment.

Can you honestly say that you were 100 percent technically "qualified" (in the strictest sense of the term) for each job you've ever taken or each promotion you received? I doubt it. Chances are, you simply had the ability to do the work. More important, perhaps, you were willing to work hard and to learn.

Education and Experience: What Do You Really Need?

The principle of limiting mandatories applies to two areas in particular: education and experience.

Before you decide automatically that the person you hire *must* have an advanced degree, ask yourself just how *necessary* that degree is. If you're looking for a salesperson, are your customers going to care one way or the other if the salesperson went to Harvard? Would you?

I'm not denying that having an advanced degree is evidence of accomplishment, and I don't want to downplay the importance of educational accomplishments. What I'm arguing against is the tendency in some companies today to use educational requirements as a means of reducing the number of applicants.

The same principle holds true for setting requirements relating to the specific experience you want to see in an applicant before you'll see that person in an interview. I can't tell you how many job-specification sheets I've seen on which somebody arbitrarily decided that in order to handle a particular job the candidate needed to have, say, five years' experience.

Why five, I've often asked myself. Why not four, or six? Isn't it possible that one person might learn in two or three years what it might take someone else five or six years to learn? Imagine if professional sports teams operated on the same principle: regardless of how talented a player was, or how well he (or she) did in college or the minor leagues, he would have to wait his turn until he'd put in a certain number of years on the bench.

Another trap to avoid is the tendency to consider only those candidates who have experience in your particular industry. Hiring only those people who have experience in your industry not only limits the field, it leads to inbreeding: you frequently end up with people who've been recycled through different companies in your industry. It's worth mentioning here that when Apple Computer was looking around for a new chief executive, the company didn't hire a computer expert—it hired a marketing specialist, John Sculley, who'd been the president of PepsiCo.

To repeat, I'm not discounting the importance of education or background. It's simply that how many years a person has gone to school or worked in a particular field doesn't necessarily reflect that person's ability to perform well in a particular job. Thus, to establish mandatories in

21

these two areas is often to eliminate from consideration the most qualified candidates.

Building in Intangibles

When the time comes to consider the less tangible attributes that affect job performance—intelligence, appearance, personality, motivation, etc.—the task of establishing hiring criteria becomes more complicated. The reason is that these criteria usually involve factors that don't relate to the job itself.

There are many such factors, but I've limited the discussion to those that prevail in most job situations.

• **You.** For better or worse, we all have our own quirks. And while it's one thing to recognize their irrationality, it's something else again to shed them.

If you're an unusually neat and organized person, you're probably not going to be happy supervising someone who is slovenly and disorganized, regardless of whatever skills that person may bring to the job. If you're a supervisor who likes to keep a tight rein on the people who work for you, you're probably not going to be happy with someone who likes to work independently. If you're the kind of supervisor who likes to give autonomy to staff members, you're not going to be happy with people who don't work well on their own.

All of which points up, once again, why it's rarely wise to have someone else draw up the hiring criteria or do the hiring for you. The issue here is not whether you are justified or unjustified in thinking the way you do, but the consequences likely to occur if you hire someone who, for whatever reason, is going to make you unhappy after being on the job for only a short time.

If you're aware of your prejudices and can overcome them, fine. But don't make the mistake of *ignoring* habits and traits that would normally make you uncomfortable, simply because you're under pressure to hire. Chances are you're not going to change your attitudes, and you will find it increasingly difficult to overlook this aspect once the pressure lifts.

• **The negatives of the job.** The ability to perform in many jobs is as much a matter of coping with the negatives as it is handling the normal pressures. You may not be able to do anything about the negatives in the job you're looking to fill, but you need to be aware of them when you're drawing up job criteria, and you need to factor in the traits necessary to deal with these negatives.

If there is an excessive amount of tedious detail in the job, for example, you obviously don't want someone who's unusually creative; the mix probably won't work. If the person you hire has to spend a great deal of time on the phone listening to complaints, you don't want anybody who has a short fuse. In fact, if you do nothing else when you're drawing up job criteria, you should force yourself to write down at least two negative aspects of the job, and then ask yourself what sort of a person would be best able to cope with them.

• **The company environment.** Some companies are highly bureaucratic, others paternal, still others free-wheeling and unstructured. So it's no surprise that certain candidates are simply better suited for certain companies.

Here again, the point is not whether a company is right or wrong in its policies or in its attitude: the company isn't likely to change, and if you hire somebody whose personality or career ambitions clash with company standards, you're inviting trouble. In fact, one of the reasons cited most frequently by employees who either quit or were fired from jobs is that the company (not the job) was simply "wrong" for them.

• **Career potential.** Make sure you understand the job opportunities before you begin looking to fill the position. And make sure you take into account the career aspirations of the person you hire.

If the job you're seeking to fill has little or no career potential and you hire someone who is anxious to carve out a career path, it won't be long before that person gets itchy and quits. This isn't to say that the person might not want the job badly at the time—but in those instances you have to do the thinking for both of you. As Gerald C. McDonough, chairman of Leaseway Transportation Corporation, pointed out to me not long ago, "When I interview a few selected candidates for an executive job, I don't

24

interview them for the job we're looking to fill, but for the next job that they should be eligible for in our company."

A Strategy for Formulating Criteria

When the time comes to actually formulate your selection criteria, the most practical strategy is to use *recent job performance* as your main criteria.

If you were satisfied with the person who held the job last, or the last couple of people who held this job, see if you can identify what it was about these people that produced the effective performance, and then put these attributes at the top of your list. Here again, be as specific as you can.

While you're at it, take another look at the background of these people—the background, that is, that directly preceded their taking the job—and see how it related to job performance. What's interesting about looking at the immediate background of employees who've already proven themselves is how often you find that such employees often *lacked* what might have seemed at the time to be an "essential" qualification. This point, of course, reinforces what I said earlier about limiting mandatories.

If the last employee was ineffective, analyze why, and then try to establish criteria that will keep you from hiring someone who will disappoint you in the same way.

25

Here again, it's not a bad idea to look at this person's background. See if you can discover, in retrospect, what it was about this person that convinced you (or somebody else) to hire him or her in the first place. Learn from your mistakes.

Be careful, though. Just as it's easy to exaggerate the importance of *positive* traits in people, so is it easy to exaggerate the importance of *negative* traits. I've known a few executives who use incredibly irrational criteria to disqualify candidates: height, weight, left-handedness, just to name just a few. Try to make certain that the negatives are definitely related to job performance.

Zeroing In

Now for what may well be the most important aspect of establishing criteria: isolating two or three characteristics that, in your view, will have the most bearing on the candidate's ability to handle the job effectively.

The characteristics I'm talking about here are not meant to be the only criteria you use in making your selection, but they *are* meant to be the principal criteria on which you base your search.

The logic here is to establish at this relatively early stage in the hiring process a sense of focus. By narrowing down the list of qualities you're looking for to those two or three that are of paramount importance, you introduce an important element of efficiency into your hiring search. You reduce the likelihood of spending a lot of time on candidates who are clearly not qualified, and you can then devote the bulk of your time to those candidates who deserve a closer look.

How Much Salary Should You Offer?

The last thing to do after you've established the basic criteria for a job is to decide how much salary you're going to offer.

In many instances your company will have an established salary schedule, in which case you won't have too much control over how much the offer will be. If, on the other hand, it's up to you to establish the salary level, here are a few guidelines to keep in mind.

First of all, don't automatically base the salary on what the *former* employee was earning. The reason: the departing employee may have been paid substantially below or above the going salary in the market.

Second, always assume that the salary of the person you hire is going to be public knowledge. If you decide to pay the new employee more than others in comparable positions are being paid, you had better be reasonably sure that existing employees won't be resentful. Consider the turmoil that often ensues when professional sports teams pay a huge salary to one player, only to have other players suddenly demand to have their contracts renegotiated.

The best policy for determining salary: find out the current market value of the job and then consider offering a little more. If you don't know the current value, consult any of the various salary studies published each year. Since 1950 my organization has published an annual guide, "Prevailing Financial and Data Processing Starting Salaries.")

Legal Ramifications

There is no law against establishing any criteria for selection that you choose, just so long as these criteria do not exclude people on the basis of race, religion, national origin, age, sex, marital status, or physical handicap not directly related to job performance.

The safest approach to take is to include in your job criteria only those factors that relate to the ability to do the job, and to give yourself a wide berth at that. Recent cases involving sex discrimination, for instance, have made it clear that you may not exclude women from employment on the basis of standards that only men can meet (usually physical capacity) unless you can prove that the standard is a true requirement and not simply your judgment.

Keep in mind, too, that a person's marital status—or the fact that one spouse or the other may have to care for young children—*cannot* be considered as a factor in the employment decision.

As Bernard Frechtman wisely points out, if you think you may be discriminating when you're drawing up job criteria, you probably are.

3 | *ON RECRUITING THE BEST CANDIDATES*

*The first step to finding something
is knowing where to look.*

The basic objective of recruiting candidates is to attract not
only numbers but quality. Too many unsuitable candidates is as big a problem as not enough suitable ones.

There is no shortage of recruiting options. You can recruit from within your own company, use recruiting services, or advertise in newspapers and magazines.

Which source is best for you will depend on several
factors: the nature of the job to be filled, the difficulty
you're likely to encounter finding good candidates, and,
most important, perhaps, the amount of time you can
afford to spend on recruiting.

But it isn't only the method you choose that's important,
it's how skillfully you utilize that method.

Let's examine the possibilities.

Recruiting in Your Own Company

All things being equal, the best place to look for candidates is within your own department or your own company.

Here's why:

First, people who've been working in your department or your company for any length of time have already proven themselves reliable, hardworking, and honest. This frees you to concentrate during screening and interviewing on the specific skills and personal attributes that relate to the job. This also eliminates the need to check references.

Second, internal candidates are already familiar with the way your company (or department) likes to operate. This means it takes less time to orient the "new" employee.

But the most important reason for choosing people from within is the positive effect it has on morale. It's well established that productivity and morale are highest in companies—and departments—committed to a promotion-from-within philosophy. And it's equally true that recruiting someone from the outside to fill a job that could conceivably be filled by someone in the company almost invariably produces friction, and can often make it very difficult for the new person to perform successfully. Indeed, if you do intend to hire someone from the outside, you risk losing one or more of the employees you've passed over. (One way to prevent this loss is to convince

32

the employees you've passed over that you still value their contribution and explain why they definitely have a bright future in the company.)

Not that there aren't pitfalls to hiring from within your own ranks. Hiring from within clearly limits the number of candidates who might handle the job well, and if you rely *only* on your company people to fill vacancies, you run the risk of building a company that is insular in its thinking.

In general, though, the advantages of recruiting from within far outweigh the pitfalls, and promotion of the people who already work for you should be fundamental to your company's recruiting policy.

Effective In-Company Recruiting

Several issues could arise when you're recruiting from within your own company, and the more aware of these issues you are, the smoother the process is likely to go.

For one thing, you need to be sensitive to the problems that could arise when you interview and turn down somebody you've known well, who has worked in the company for a long time. It's the rare business relationship that isn't bruised by rejections of this nature. When this situation arises, respond the same as you would if you were dealing with a passed-over employee: assure the employee that while the "fit" may have been wrong, he or she is a person of ability and still important to the company.

33

You also need to be sensitive to the possibility that one department might not appreciate the fact that another department is "pirating" its good people. This is why it's important that you or whoever is doing the hiring go through channels when you are looking inside your company, although which channels and in which order are debatable and could vary depending on the people and company politics involved.

Most personnel professionals recommend that if you are a manager and you have your eye on somebody in the company, you should first approach the personnel department. The reasoning: the personnel department sees the "big picture" of people in your company and, additionally, may know something about the candidate that could influence your decision.

There are exceptions. If you work closely with the person's supervisor, for instance, I see no reason why you shouldn't approach the supervisor first. And just not out of courtesy, either. Here, too, the supervisor could tell you something about the candidate that could change your thinking before you go any further.

In either case, never approach the individual you're considering prematurely. It's conceivable that after you approach this person, you might change your mind. In the meantime, you've raised the hopes of that employee, and because you changed your mind, you could create so much disappointment that he or she might decide to leave the company.

Job Posting

More and more companies now make it a policy to keep employees informed of job openings by posting selected openings on bulletin boards or in company publications. The practice is known as "job posting," and it makes sense on several counts.

Not only does posting jobs increase the number of qualified candidates, it's good for employee morale: notices of job openings communicate to employees that management is serious about promoting from within, and give employees a broader view of career potential in the company. Job posting also helps management identify those employees who are the most interested in career advancement, and because it encourages all employees to bid for jobs, job posting is good insurance against future job-discrimination claims.

If you're going to use job posting, make sure to formulate a policy for handling applications that protects employees who would rather their supervisors didn't find out that they were looking elsewhere in the company. Whether supervisors should or shouldn't be informed when one of their staff members is applying for another job within the company is something you'll have to decide for yourself. The policy followed by some companies is to inform the supervisors of only those employees who become serious contenders for the job.

When Management Works with Personnel

A strong, well-run personnel department is extremely important to a company's overall hiring strategy. It isn't only that good personnel people are well versed in all the legal aspects of hiring and can greatly simplify the search for management by narrowing down the selection to the most qualified people—a good personnel department can also help management get a better grasp of overall needs and help individual managers pick better people.

Even so, personnel departments take a lot of heat in many companies—sometimes justifiably and sometimes not. Complaints vary from company to company, but the criticism you hear most often is essentially this: the people in personnel are too "credentials-oriented" and are not sufficiently tuned in to the realistic needs of middle- to higher-level positions. The criteria they use, the argument goes, often eliminate from consideration people who could do a good job in favor of candidates who have the credentials, but may lack the innate ability or motivation needed to do the job well.

The fact is, as most personnel executives will admit, and as our Burke surveys clearly show, personnel people rarely make the final decision for most jobs. The function of the personnel department in most companies is to provide suitable choices for management; the actual hiring decision is made by the candidate's potential boss.

What's more, the ability of the personnel department to

provide suitable choices is largely dependent on the person who is doing the actual hiring. In many cases, managers who are critical of the caliber of candidates arriving for interviews have only themselves to blame. The reason: they may not have communicated clearly enough to personnel just what sort of person was required for the job. "Our biggest problem," the personnel director of one "Fortune 500" company complained to me not long ago, "is that not enough of the people in management know what they're looking for. They have a general idea of the job requirements, but they don't appreciate the intangibles, and in many instances they create arbitrary and unnecessary specifications. It isn't until we've sent them a half dozen or so people that they begin to get a clearer picture of what they really need."

So principle number one in working with the personnel department is this: do whatever you can to help your personnel department do its job better. An intelligently written job description is a must. But it's also worth the time in many situations to discuss your needs in detail with the personnel person who is responsible for the search. Such a discussion could well open up your eyes to aspects of the job you weren't aware of and lead you to develop a better job description.

It's important, too, that you do more than simply reject unsuitable candidates sent to you by the personnel department, but that you always give some rationale for the rejection. That way, the person you're working with has a clearer idea of whom to send you the next time around. A good personnel director isn't going to ram anybody down your throat, but you can't expect people to read your mind: you have to paint a clear enough picture of what you're looking for so that whoever you're working with in personnel can adjust his or her own thinking to meet your needs.

Finally, to guard against the possibility that the personnel department may be turning down candidates who might turn out to be well suited for the job, ask them to show you the applications or résumés of a number of "rejects"—candidates ruled out because they didn't meet some of the standards for the job. I'm willing to bet that you'll find one or two people from this group whom you'd like to interview, and who could turn out to be top contenders for the job.

Personal Recommendations

You shouldn't hesitate to call on personal contacts for leads on people who might make good candidates, but neither should you treat these recommendations any differently from those for candidates you get from other sources.

The main reason for going to people you know is that you may have confidence in their suggestions—particularly if your contact is in the same field as the candidate. It's been my experience that good people in a particular field are usually excellent judges of who's good and who isn't good in their field.

However, there are also risks to this strategy. When a friend or an already proven employee recommends someone, there's sometimes a tendency to slack off a little in your search, or else to "prehire" the recommended person before you've had a chance to conduct an interview.

There's also a risk that the person giving you the recommendation wants to do the candidate a favor—a favor that could prove to be at your expense. This risk is documented by one of our Burke findings, which indicates that friends of candidates are often less than candid in giving complete reference information. On balance, however, as in the case of recruiting from your own company, the advantages of using contacts outweigh the relative risks. You simply need to take a few precautionary steps. Here are three specific suggestions:

1. Interview the contact. To overcome the possibility that the person being recommended by a friend or contact might not be suitable, "interview" the friend or contact first. Spend some time asking some of the same questions you might ask the candidate. This way, you may discover that your contact doesn't know enough about the candidate's abilities or background to make a strong recommendation. The contact may be acting, in fact, like a marriage broker, simply getting the two of you together to see what happens.

2. Don't assume too much. Make sure you evaluate

candidates recommended to you by people you trust as objectively as you evaluate all other candidates. It's worth mentioning that less than 50 percent of our Burke survey respondents thought it was good practice to hire somebody on the basis of a personal recommendation, and about 25 percent advised against it.

3. Don't ignore references. Regardless of who makes the recommendation, don't make the mistake of being any less diligent in your reference checking. I can remember years ago hiring a young man who had been recommended by a friend of mine whom I hadn't seen for several years. Because I knew the friend pretty well, it never dawned on me to check the young man's references. But after a while I had reason to suspect the honesty of the statements the young man had given me. I did some investigating on my own and found that he'd recently served time in jail for embezzlement and there was a likelihood that he'd be indicted again.

Recruiting Services

Recruiting services are referred to in any number of different ways—personnel agencies, executive recruiters, headhunters, etc.—but all serve essentially the same function: they find, screen, and recommend candidates. If they're good, they find you more qualified candidates in less time than you're likely to find on your own, and they help to expedite the overall hiring process.

There are several advantages to working with a good recruiting service. First, you're spared the time—and money—it takes to advertise, to screen résumés, and to handle preliminary interviews. Second, you can keep your company's name and the job opening confidential until the time comes to begin the actual interviews. Finally, the only people you eventually interview when you use a recruiting service are people who are qualified to handle the job.

Because I've been in the personnel-recruitment business myself for more than thirty-five years, I'm hardly an objective observer, but I'm not unaware of the failings of our industry. It's no secret that not everybody in our industry operates according to the highest professional standards, and that when you work with some services you end up complicating—not simplifying—your hiring procedures.

Fortunately, however, the bad apples in our industry are in the minority, particularly when it comes to the firms that have been in business for some time. The track record of quality recruiting services underscores the valuable role they play in a productive hiring strategy: if the need didn't exist, the recruiting industry wouldn't be as big as it has become.

The Options

All personnel services—whether they call themselves recruiters, executive search specialists, or personnel agencies—do essentially the same thing, with varying degrees of overlap. All search for specific people to fit specific jobs. All personnel services maintain files of candidates who, in their judgment, are suitable for job assignments that they are likely to get in the future. All personnel services advertise in newspapers and trade journals to help locate specific people. And all the better services rely on their reputations to attract the better candidates.

The reason I emphasize the "all" is that some people put "executive search" specialists or "recruiters" or "headhunters" in a special category, assuming, for instance, that "recruiters" handle only positions that call for six-figure salaries, or that recruiters will submit for consideration to a client *only* a candidate who is employed. Both of these perceptions are myths.

It's also a myth that companies who describe themselves as recruiters do not advertise for candidates. Many do: they simply run blind ads. And it's a myth, too, that recruiters deal with clients strictly on a retainer basis. Most executive search firms, if pressed, would concede that under certain situations they have agreed to accept a contingency fee from clients, either in whole or in part.

42

That's one version of the myth.

The other version of the myth is that personnel services that do not refer to themselves as "search firms" or "recruiters" are not equipped to handle six-figure positions, deal only with the unemployed, never get a retainer from a client, rely exclusively on advertising to get job candidates—and, for that matter, work for and collect their fee from the candidate.

Again, all myths. The fact is, many personnel services deal routinely with high-salary positions and place many more currently employed candidates than candidates who are unemployed. Some personnel agencies work on retainers, and the good ones, far from relying solely on advertising, will do whatever is appropriate to find the right person for a client. They search out individuals and they maintain confidential files of acceptable candidates. Finally, very few agencies, particularly those dealing with middle- and upper-level jobs, receive any money from applicants.

I'm not saying that you won't find certain differences between certain "recruiters" and personnel agencies, only that these differences are not nearly as great as some would lead you to believe. The important decision, in the end, is not whether to use a company that calls itself an agency or a recruiter. The important thing is that whomever you use should have a proven reputation and be a company in which you have confidence.

Setting Up the Arrangement

Regardless of whom you use, make sure you understand the financial arrangement before you begin to interview candidates sent to you. The personnel service should make the terms known to you in writing, and should disclose any other hidden charges (for example, phone and travel expenses that you didn't agree upon) that may arise when payment is due.

I would also recommend that you use specialized personnel services to fill positions calling for a specialized occupation, profession, or industry. Specialists not only have greater access than generalists to better people in the field, they have the ability to evaluate the quality of potential candidates. And because they are able to choose from a larger pool of talent, specialists increase the odds of getting better people.

If it's practical, visit the personnel service's office. Meet as many of the people in the firm as you can. Take note of little things, such as how the receptionist greets applicants. Try to put yourself in the shoes of a job seeker using that office. Ask yourself how you would feel walking into that office. And don't hesitate to ask them for their references. Talk to other clients the service has worked for, and talk to other people in your company who may have worked with any personnel service you're thinking of using.

Once you're comfortable with a recruiter, make sure you

communicate exactly what you're looking for, and take advantage of the recruiter's experience to help you decide if your employment objectives are realistic at the salary you're prepared to pay. We've found consistently in our offices a direct correlation between the success of the placement and the amount of useful information we were able to draw from the employer.

Communicate in as detailed a manner as possible what you believe your needs are and what the employee who ultimately gets the job will be expected to do. Be prepared as well to give enough feedback after each interview so that the recruiter is in an increasingly stronger position, as the search proceeds, to locate and select the people likely to satisfy your needs.

Should You Give Exclusives?

More often than not it's a good idea to deal with just one recruiting service for any given job search. If you agree to pay the recruiter a substantial fee in advance, you're almost forced into an exclusive arrangement since your company has made a cash investment in the success of the search. But if you agree to pay a small retainer, or none at all, exclusivity is definitely an advantage to the company provided you are convinced they have the proven ability to produce qualified candidates. Here's my reasoning:

If a personnel service understands that it has an exclusive, it is bound to consider the client with whom it has this arrangement most important. The agency, after all, is almost assured that it will fill the position and earn the fee.

Let's assume, on the other hand, that three personnel services are working on the same position and that each has an equal opportunity to fill the job. Given that the odds in this instance are two to one against the agency filling the job, the service must now pursue two additional searches for roughly the same projected fee.

My strategy, if I were dealing with a personnel service on any sort of contingency, would be to offer the exclusive with the understanding that at any time, if I became dissatisfied, I could let them know, and proceed to choose another service. (I would then give *that* personnel service an exclusive.)

Recruiting Through Advertising

Advertising is probably the most widely used recruiting strategy in business today, and is one of the many ways we recruit candidates at Robert Half International's independent offices. And because our combined advertising budget is about $15 million per year in newspaper, magazine, radio, and TV, I think I'm in a good position to discuss it as a recruiting method.

The chief value of advertising is that few other methods

are likely to draw as many candidates. On the other hand, the majority of the candidates attracted by ads are not even close to becoming contenders.

If you choose to advertise, you need to be careful about *where* you advertise and *when* you advertise, and you have to focus, more than most people seem willing to, on *how* you word your ads.

Where—and When—to Place the Ads

You will usually draw the biggest response by placing ads on Sundays, and in newspapers that carry the most employment advertising.

But there are sometimes reasons for advertising on different days of the week and in other media. Most of the Robert Half offices, for instance, advertise primarily on Sundays, but we also place ads in the *Wall Street Journal* (primarily on Tuesdays, because that is the big day for employment advertising in the *Journal*).

If you're looking for a specialist, consider a trade publication that caters to specialists in the field. We advertise extensively in financial and data processing publications and are generally pleased with the results. And if your company is located in a suburban area, don't overlook local papers, particularly when you're trying to fill less specialized positions.

I should mention also that we've found radio and televi-

47

sion advertising to be an increasingly useful tool for attracting some of the best people (assuming your budget allows for these media). We've found that the morning and evening drive times on the best-rated stations are the most productive on radio. With television, we've had the best results with local interview shows, particularly those that run on Sunday morning.

Size and Appearance

How large you make the ad will depend primarily on how much you think you can afford to spend. The larger the ad, the greater the response, and the more substantial your company appears to job seekers.

If you're going to take out a display ad, make sure it looks good. Even though most newspapers have their own layout departments, have a professional graphics designer design the ad and assemble the mechanical. The extra money you spend will pay for itself in a larger response from good candidates.

Open Versus Blind Ads

Unless you have a strong reason for doing otherwise, avoid "blind" ads—ads in which you show only a box number to respond to.

There are two good reasons. Surveys have shown, first of all, that job seekers are often mistrustful (as they should be) of blind ads. Second, blind ads rarely draw responses from currently employed people. It's simply too big a risk for people who are secure in their present jobs. There's always the possibility that the response to a blind ad could directly or indirectly get into the hands of the respondent's employer.

Who *does* answer blind ads? In most cases, three categories of job seekers: people who are unemployed, people who sense that they're *about* to be unemployed, and people who are indiscreet enough to send personal and confidential information to a box number.

Those companies who deliberately choose to omit their names from advertisements usually do so for one of four reasons:

1. They're looking outside the company for personnel and don't want others in the company to find out about it.
2. The company has a bad personnel reputation and its name is likely to discourage applicants.
3. They don't have a specific job in mind but are scouting to see who's available just in case.
4. The company doesn't want to tip off the fact that it's thinking of moving or it's developing a new product line.

By the way, if you feel it is absolutely *necessary* to keep your company's name out of the ad, don't use a post office box number. To find out the name of the person or company to whom a post office box number has been assigned, all one needs to do is call the post office.

Wording the Ad

The way you describe the position could have a greater bearing than you may think on the response you receive, and in particular, on the quality of that response. Give it thought.

As in any advertisement, your goal is to elicit quality responses. This means that in addition to supplying the basic information about the job—the duties, the salary, the location, etc.—the ad should have a strong element of "sell."

The amount of "sell" in an ad is not measured by how many adjectives are in the ad, and I'm not recommending that you glorify or in any way misrepresent the job, simply to elicit more responses. To the contrary, your ad should be truthful in every respect. If not, you could leave yourself open to fraudulent-advertising charges.

What's important for now is the "story" behind the ad and how you orchestrate that story.

The headline and the opening. As in all advertising, the function of a heading is to attract the reader's attention.

The most important headline element for employment

advertising is the title of the job—vice-president of finance, sales manager, civil engineer, retail controller, traffic manager, programmer–COBOL, property-tax manager, secretary, etc. But immediately following the headline should be an opening that spells out the prime benefit of the job. Assuming that the greatest benefit of the job is salary, put it in fairly large type, right under the headline.

In classified advertising the opening is important for yet another reason: it will determine where the ad appears. Newspapers generally run their classified ads alphabetically, based on the headline or the first word in the ad. So if you are advertising for an assistant bookkeeper, make sure the word "bookkeeper" appears before "assistant."

One other thought about titles. Some companies use titles internally that don't accurately reflect the exact nature of the job. I once had a client who was looking for an "auditor," but when I began asking questions about the job, it turned out that the job was really that of controller. The reason for the confusion is that the person who'd held this job for the past twenty years had always been called an "auditor," even though he functioned as a controller. The reason this distinction was so important is that an opening for an auditor would not draw interest from the kind of people who could handle the job.

Concentrate in particular on the first sentence of the ad. Use the "benefit" to key the story. Make sure the first sentence of the ad communicates the key selling point of the job. Here are some good examples:

World-renowned museum looking for astute individual to manage our financial affairs. [*This opening sells the prestige of working for a fine museum.*]

A rapidly growing restaurant chain is seeking a manager who is anxious to take on more responsibility. [*This opening sells the career potential.*]

A small but dynamic advertising agency that specializes in travel accounts is looking for an administrative assistant who likes variety and doesn't mind the pressures of deadlines. [*This opening sells the glamour of working in travel.*]

The body of the ad. Apart from capturing the interest of the reader with an opening that has some "sell" to it, make sure your ad spells out a sufficient amount of basic information about the job. At the very least, the ad should communicate the following:

1. Nature of the job
2. Kind of company
3. Location of company
4. Salary
5. Growth potential (if there is any)

As I cautioned earlier, don't misrepresent the job. I know of a company that ran a blind ad in which it described itself as a "growth" company, even though the company was operating under Chapter 11 of bankruptcy. A job seeker was called in for an interview, found out the truth, and reported the company to the attorney general.

I know of another situation in which a company included the phrase "light travel" among the list of functions in its ad. The job, as it turned out, called for very heavy travel, and when the man who eventually took the job was fired because he didn't want to travel that much, he threatened to sue and was prepared to use the ad to back up his case. The company was forced to settle.

Apart from being honest, be selective in your details. There's no need to list functions that everyone associates with a particular position. It's taken for granted that a magazine art director will be responsible for layouts and that a secretary will have to do typing.

In place of this obvious information, indicate tasks or responsibilities that may be unique to this position— unique in relation to the same position in other companies. Is there more responsibility than normal, more travel, more opportunity for advancement?

Finally, avoid empty adjectives. If you're going to describe an opportunity as "exciting," give some indication of what makes the job exciting. And avoid obvious exaggerations: phrases like "fantastic opportunity" not only don't sell, they put people on their guard.

A few other principles to keep in mind when writing an ad:

1. Go easy on the abbreviations. Using abbreviations can save you money, but when the abbreviations begin interfering with your ability to understand what the job is, it's time to stop. Ads that have unfamiliar abbreviations tend to draw poorly. A good rule to follow: use only abbreviations that are very obvious (such as "exp." and "mfr."), and try not to put two abbreviations back to back. In other words, avoid the following:

> Tp flt pro with dem.
> ab and exptse to orgze,
> admitsr, the ،
> Int. acct. fctin for
> con. prod. gi.

2. Don't be afraid to personalize. No law forbids you from using personal pronouns like "we" and "you" in an ad. Look at the following two examples and decide for yourself which one would most likely draw more responses.

> Dynamic oppty with blue chip natural resources giant. Become involved in international financial reporting, foreign exchange, letters of credit, securities, and special projects. 2+ yrs public/private best. CPA or MBA preferred.

> We are a blue chip natural resources giant offering a dynamic opportunity to join our international accounting staff. You will become involved in international financial reporting, foreign exchange, letters of credit, securities, and special projects. We'd prefer a CPA or MBA with at least two years public or private accounting experience.

3. Don't get carried away. Use simple, sincere, and factual language. Let the job—not the words you use—do the selling.

Instead of:

> As an eminent leader in its industry, Prestige Corporation has a truly outstanding career opportunity in its fabulous Burbank location for a uniquely personable individual to train our valued customers in the efficient use of our sensational preprogrammed left-handed word processing system.

This:

> Prestige Corporation, an industry leader, has an outstanding career opportunity in its Burbank location for a personable individual who will train customers to use our preprogrammed left-handed word processing system.

4. Edit judiciously. When you need to cut down on words to save money, start with unnecessary articles ("the," "a," "an," etc.), or eliminate the subject of a sentence when it is clearly understood. Your high-school English teacher might not approve, but it's accepted practice in employment advertising to edit in this manner.

Instead of:

> We are a division of a "Fortune 500"
> consumer products company, with an
> outstanding opportunity in our Market-
> ing Department, created by a recent
> promotion to a management position.

This:

> Division of "Fortune 500" consumer
> products company has outstanding
> opportunity in Marketing Dept. created
> by recent promotion into a management
> position.

5. Eliminate the subject when it is clearly understood.

Instead of:

> The candidate must have superior orga-
> nizational skills.

This:

> Must have superior organizational
> skills.

Legal Ramifications

Several legal issues arise when you are recruiting for candidates. Let's look briefly at each of them.

First of all, you must be scrupulously careful that any advertising you do is not worded in any way that might be construed as discriminatory based upon race, color, religion, national origin, age, sex, marital status, or handicap. It's no longer acceptable, for example, to advertise for a "Gal Friday." (Some people use "Gal/Man," but I dislike the contrivance. "Secretary" or "administrative assistant" would be better.) Indeed, you should take great pains to exclude from your ads any words that might discourage members of either sex from applying.

The same principle holds true for age, except that in some states, curiously enough, you can run an ad that reads "40 and above." This is because federal law only protects candidates between the ages of forty and seventy. The safest policy, however, is to eliminate any reference to age (such as, "recent college grad"), not just because of the legal implications but also because in most positions age should not be a factor in job selection.

Two areas in which it is legal to indicate specifications are education and experience, but you still have to be careful about how you word the experience requirement. To say "2 years' experience" and nothing else could leave you open to a charge that you've set an age requirement. If you're going to establish an experience requirement, it has to be in a *specific* area, such as "3 years' sales experience."

Even here, however, you have to be careful. In certain professions the number of women or minority candidates has only recently begun to increase. So limiting applicants to people who've been in a field for, say, ten years *could* leave you open to a lawsuit. The safest policy: keep your language neutral, non–age restrictive, and pertinent to the job requirements.

Apart from wording that might be considered discriminatory, refrain from making any promises in your ads ("permanent career," "secure," etc.) that could get you into trouble if it becomes necessary later on to terminate the employment.

4 ON EVALUATING RÉSUMÉS

A résumé is a balance sheet without any liabilities.

Résumés are a necessary evil.

They're tedious to plow through, and they rarely yield an accurate picture of a candidate. I've read thousands of résumés in my career, and I have yet to find any significant correlation between the quality of a résumé and the likelihood that the candidate who wrote it will turn out to be a successful employee. Some of the most talented candidates I've ever come across simply refused to spend time on their résumés, and some of the weakest candidates I've interviewed prepared résumés worthy in their own right of a Pulitzer Prize.

Yet, for better or for worse, a résumé remains one of the means of choosing which applicants should be interviewed and which shouldn't. And for this reason alone, reading through résumés is one job you don't want to delegate. Later in this section I'll suggest some ways you can streamline the process, but for now let me stress the basic principle of reading résumés: that it isn't enough to simply *read* a résumé. You have to read between the lines. You have to look beyond the facts presented and draw an added measure of insight that will enable you to decide whether or not the candidate should be interviewed.

What to Look For

The main thing to be sensitive to when you're screening résumés are the signs—often hidden—that indicate the qualities that make for a successful employee. These qualities are often independent of the specific information the résumé provides. In some instances, the candidate won't even be aware of them.

Here are some examples of what I mean.

•   **Signs of achievement and profit-mindedness.** In every résumé you read, look for evidence of achievement and accomplishment. The rationale here is basic: the best indicator of successful future performance is successful past performance.

Given the relationship between past performance and future performance, be wary of candidates whose résumés reflect a number of lateral moves—moves that brought no more responsibility or money. The exceptions: candidates who may have made lateral moves for good reasons, such as changing careers or taking jobs to get off the unemployment line.

While you're tracking down evidence of accomplishment, see if you can sense, from how the candidate has described specific functions or responsibilities, if the candidate is profit-oriented. See how often the résumé draws attention to functions that had a direct bearing on the earnings of the company: how specific actions produced sales increases or improved efficiency.

True, clever candidates will deliberately highlight this aspect of the résumé, knowing that accomplishments are of interest to performance-minded interviewers. Don't worry. You'll have time during the interview to focus on those functions and to decide for yourself whether the candidate is truly profit-oriented or is exaggerating the value of his or her contributions.

•   **Patterns of stability and career direction.** See what the résumé tells you about the candidate's stability and career direction, but be careful how you interpret the pattern.

Some personnel specialists automatically eliminate all candidates who have changed jobs frequently over the past several years, but I never turn down candidates for this reason—not until I've delved into the reason for the job jumping. The fact that they have been hired so many times indicates that there must be something attractive about them. I know one sales manager who deliberately seeks out such people. He figures that anybody who is good enough to repeatedly sell himself or herself at an interview has good sales potential.

Yes, frequent changes *can* indicate instability (and I

myself have always been wary of *excessive* job jumping), but if the candidate has bettered himself or herself with each change, you can usually assume a reasonably high level of competence. The only thing you have to be wary of is whether the job you're looking to fill is challenging enough to put an end to the pattern of frequent changes.

• **Specifics in job descriptions.** The less specific candidates are when they are describing what they did, the more likely they are trying to inflate the importance of what was actually accomplished. A résumé may read "supervised a department," but you have no way of knowing how big that department was unless the résumé also specifies the number of people supervised.

Be sensitive to how specific—or general—the résumé is when it talks about increases in sales, profits, or productivity. Here again, you'll be able to explore these areas in more depth during the interview. But if you find yourself with a cornucopia of candidates, give the nod to those who spell out their achievements and accomplishments.

• **Willingness to work hard.** How hard a candidate is likely to work once hired is next to impossible to predict from a résumé alone. But there are some generally reliable signs that indicate whether a candidate has this quality.

I've always favored candidates whose tasks and responsibilities in each of their jobs went beyond the normal parameters of the job. This usually indicates people who aren't locked into a "job-description" mentality. I also like candidates whose leisure activities include volunteer work for organizations; such involvement usually indicates a higher than average level of industriousness.

What to Be Wary Of

Just as there is information in résumés that can indicate a candidate well worth an interview, there are signs that suggest otherwise. I wouldn't entirely rule out any candidate on the strength of these signs alone, but when you're faced with an overwhelming number of possible applicants, here are some of the areas in which to do some weeding out.

• **Lengthy descriptions of education.** Outside of any specific degrees or certificates a candidate may have earned, little else in the education section should occupy your attention. Lengthy descriptions of seminars or specific courses may not be all that important, and are usually written by candidates who lack the appropriate educational background. The degrees listed are important, but more as evidence of accomplishment than proof of intelligence—particularly if the degrees are irrelevant to the job.

• **Obvious gaps in background.** Candidates who've made a career out of job jumping will frequently try to conceal this fact by preparing their résumés in the so-called functional form, which eliminates chronological details. The fact that a candidate has prepared such a

63

résumé doesn't necessarily mean he or she isn't worth a closer look. The candidate could well be a person who has been out of work simply because he or she has been very selective about offers.

• **Trivia in the "personal" section.** Candidates who puff up the "personal" sections with a long list of interests and hobbies could inadvertently be telling you one of two things: one, they are weak in experience and skills; two, they have such a busy leisure life, they may not have enough time for the job.

• **An overabundance of qualifiers.** A résumé that's filled with phrases such as "knowledge of," "had exposure to," "assisted with," etc., usually indicates that the candidate hasn't had the hands-on experience in these areas that you might be looking for.

• **Sour grapes.** You don't often run into résumés that have a bitter or self-righteous tone, but when you do, save yourself some time and put this résumé at the bottom of the pile or in the wastebasket. If anger shows through a résumé, chances are it's going to surface on the job. And if a candidate is shortsighted enough to be critical of his or her past employer in a résumé, it could happen again—but this time with your company taking the brunt of the criticism.

• **Slick résumé.** By "slick" I'm talking about gimmicky devices (a pretentious typeface, an odd color) that make the résumé stand out from all the rest. You'll have to use your own judgment, but I've found, in general, that candidates who rely on gimmicky résumés are rarely as interesting as their résumés.

Streamlining the Sorting Process

Résumé reading is best approached in small sips. When you try to digest too many at one sitting, you lose the ability to distinguish one from another.

Here are a few suggestions to help you streamline the process.

First of all, plan at the outset to divide the résumés into three groups: (1) the "definites" (people you definitely want to interview), (2) the "maybes" (people who could conceivably work out), and (3) the "nos" (people whose background, as indicated by the résumé, shows they are clearly unqualified).

Second, when you read through the résumés the first time and you come across a "definite," put that résumé in the "definite" pile. (You'll have time later, if necessary, to cull that pile if there are too many people in it.)

Third, get into the habit of reading *first* the part of the résumé that deals with experience. Better still, read the résumé from bottom to top (the theory being that most candidates put the least flattering information at the end of the résumé).

65

Finally, go through the "maybes" and choose at least one or two of them to interview. Doing so will test your objectivity and help you determine the validity of your job criteria. If you find your "maybes" are stronger than your "definites," it's time to rethink your criteria.

When Others Do the Screening

Certain jobs draw so many applicants that you have no choice but to have someone else assist in the screening.

If this is the case, I have two pieces of advice. The first is try to find a specialist—someone familiar with the specific occupation, profession, or industry—to do the screening, making sure that you get together with that person to set some basic guidelines as to who should and shouldn't be eliminated from consideration. Personnel services are often useful in this regard. They'll do all the preliminary screening and then submit the résumés of only those candidates who warrant serious consideration.

Second, no matter who does the screening, make sure you see a representative sampling of the résumés that have been rejected—maybe 10 percent. Read through these résumés yourself. If you find that you would have rejected them too, you can rest comfortably in the knowledge that there are few undiscovered winners in the "reject" pile. But if you find some résumés that would have made your "definite" or "maybe" pile, it's clear that the screening hasn't done what it was meant to do, and that you have some résumé reading to do on your own.

Some Thoughts About Application Forms

I haven't dwelled on application forms, not because applications aren't important but because different companies have different philosophies about how long the application form should be and what information it should elicit from the candidate.

Let me review briefly, however, some purely legal points about applications.

There's little need, of course, to remind you that no question on the form should touch upon a prospective employee's race, color, religion, national origin, age, sex, marital status, or, in most instances, disability. But if it's not already there, the application form your company uses should state that your company is an Equal Employment Opportunity Employer and that you do not discriminate on the basis of race, color, religion, national origin, age, sex, marital status, or handicap.

Another suggestion: your application should contain a statement that makes it clear that employment will be solely "at will" and not for a lifetime or specific period of time. Here's an example:

> I understand and agree that this employment application, by itself or together with other company documents or policy statements, does not create a contract of employment. I also understand that I may voluntarily leave or be terminated at any time and for any reason.

This statement should be in bold type and should be just above the applicant's signature line.

5	# ON TESTING AS A SCREENING TOOL

*It's the rare test that can't be
beaten.*

The ultimate value of tests (psychological tests, in particular) as a tool in hiring is one of the more debatable issues in recruitment, so I wasn't surprised that our Burke survey question on the subject found respondents split almost down the middle. Some 39 percent of respondents felt that psychological testing was "helpful" in selection, but 41 percent felt otherwise (20 percent had no opinion one way or the other). What's interesting, however, is that only a small proportion of respondents who took either position felt strongly about it one way or the other.

Tests in and of themselves come in a number of varieties and are designed to test any number of skills, attributes, and personal characteristics. There are achievement tests designed to measure knowledge or skills in specific areas (data processing, etc.); aptitude tests designed to measure a candidate's innate capacities in specific areas; intelligence tests designed to measure a candidate's ability to think and reason; interest tests, which are meant to indicate what the candidate likes or doesn't like to do; and, finally, psychological tests, which are meant to give you a look inside the candidate's psyche.

I have never been a strong advocate of testing as a selection tool, with one notable exception: when you are testing for a specific skill, such as word processing. Yes, I like the idea of having objective criteria to use in selection, but I have reservations about the overall validity of the results. Except for specific achievement tests, I've yet to see a test that a shrewd candidate couldn't see through. I've seen tests for sales personnel in which a typical question asks whether the person taking the test would prefer to "spend an evening reading a book" or to "go to a party." You don't have to be a genius to figure out which of these answers is more likely to enhance the chance of getting hired.

It could be argued, of course, that a candidate smart enough to see through the test is someone worth hiring, but that's not the issue: the issue is whether testing is worth the bother for most companies. I don't think so.

Problems with testing go beyond the ability of candidates to manipulate the answers. Some people, for instance, simply do not take tests well. Consequently, they are knocked out of the running for reasons that may have nothing to do with their ability to perform the job. Many tests, particularly those that were developed prior to EEO legislation, are blatantly discriminatory. And companies that rely on tests as the *chief* selection criteria have a tendency to become stereotyped in their managerial styles: they wind up hiring people who think too much alike.

Then, too, the validity of many of the psychological tests commonly used in business today has yet to be established. The *true* measure of validity would be to compare the job performance of candidates who fared well on the test with the performance of a comparable number of candidates who fared poorly. To my knowledge, very few, if any, evaluations of this kind have ever been carried out. The reason is that the people who fared poorly are usually not hired, and hence there is no way to measure their job performance.

Finally, some of the tests—the personality tests, in particular—are so complex, you need a specialist to interpret the results. This usually involves outside specialists. This slows down and complicates the hiring process, and also makes it more expensive.

On the other hand, I'm obliged to report that a number of excellent companies rely extensively on psychological testing and appear happy with the results. I know of a West Coast food company that has been using psychological tests in the hiring of sales personnel since the late 1970s and reports that the tests do a much better job of revealing the "true" candidate than the interview does. The rationale behind the tests they use is that successful sales-

71

people tend to have similar characteristics, chief among them resiliency (they bounce back quickly) and a strong drive to persuade other people to accept their point of view.

I recently learned of a "Fortune 500" corporation that has found a direct correlation between how well candidates for sales positions do on a particular test and how long these people stay with the company once they're hired. (I should add, however, that it took the company nearly seven years to develop this test.)

Undoubtedly, then, testing may have its place in selection, just so long as you have some means of validating the results. But before you launch a testing program, here are some points to keep in mind.

First, there are some complex legal ramifications of tests, as will be indicated. Make yourself aware of them.

Second, choose the tests—and testing companies—with care. Take the time to ensure that the tests you use are keyed to your particular needs, and keep in mind that most of the people who run testing companies will advise you that the results of testing should never be the determining factor in hiring and should always be accompanied by interviewing and reference checking. I'm thinking in particular of personality tests designed to reflect a candidate's suitability to a particular field, and I'm thinking, too, about the accountants I know and how *different* their personalities are. It's hard for me to imagine any test that could take into account these differences.

Legal Implications

If you're not careful, testing can be a legal minefield, and it's up to you—not the testing company—to make sure that whatever testing procedure you use meets fundamental criteria established by the Equal Employment Opportunity legislation.

There are two key considerations here.

First, consistent with all EEO legislation, any of the tests you use as part of hiring must be related to the specific job for which the candidate has applied (as opposed to a test that simply measures general characteristics). If pressed, you need to be able to demonstrate that the results of the test or the testing procedure you use represent a reasonable way of predicting job performance.

Second, the nature of the questions themselves cannot reduce the chances of minorities or women being hired. You must be able to demonstrate that responses to any question do not eliminate from consideration a disproportionate number of candidates in any single group.

These are hazy distinctions, I grant you, but the point to bear in mind is this: if you're ever called upon to defend against the charge that the test reduced the chances of hiring a minority or female candidate, you'll have to show that a definite correlation exists between high test performance and high job performance. To repeat, the test must be job-related, not person-related.

73

*The job interview is a two-way
street: the company interviewing
the candidate, and the candidate
interviewing the company.*

The job interview (sometimes referred to as the "selection
interview") is the most familiar aspect of hiring, and the
most controversial as well. Virtually everyone relies to
some extent on interviewing to help them make the hiring
choice (an estimated 160 million such interviews take
place every year in the U.S.), but even those employment
specialists who rely heavily on the interview concede its
shortcomings.

Consider what you're up against.

For an hour, or less, you sit down with somebody you've
never seen before to elicit enough information and develop enough of a general sense of the person to make a
decision that could have a profound impact on you, your
company, and the candidate.

Compounding this difficulty is the fact that job interviews do not represent a typical work setting. This means
that candidates being interviewed are not necessarily pre-

senting an accurate picture of how they are likely to perform on the job: interviews often reflect how candidates present themselves during an interview.

Finally, the people you're interviewing have their own objectives—namely, to try their best to give you the answers they think you want to hear.

So much for the negative side of the picture.

The positive side is that the interview, if you know how to handle it, is the single most *useful* tool in the entire hiring process—useful in the sense that it can produce a picture of the candidate that you can't get from a résumé, an application, or references. The problem, though, is that you can't take the job interview for granted. You need to recognize its possibilities and its limitations, and you should approach each interview with a sense of purpose, and with an understanding of how best to get the information you require.

The Essence of Interviewing

Skillful interviewing is not, as some people seem to think, a "seat of the pants" skill. Yes, there is a common-sense element to interviewing, but interviewing someone with an eye toward hiring is a unique situation with a unique set of demands. It requires not only a systematic approach but a combination of skills that most people do not come by naturally.

The biggest mistake you can make as an interviewer is to try to "wing it"—that is, to approach the interview as if it were a conversation, with the purpose being that you and the candidate "get to know each other."

Such an approach—more widespread than you may think—virtually guarantees failure. You may know people who have a knack for choosing good employees and whose style of interviewing seems unstructured and offhand. But don't confuse style with approach. I know such people, and I know how hard they try to *seem* unstructured and offhand. It's their way of putting the candidate at ease and of eliciting responses that candidates don't plan on making.

A basic principle of successful interviewing is: recognize that interviewing candidates isn't something you can approach casually and that there are specific objectives in each interview, and ways to go about accomplishing these objectives.

Another important principle that is often overlooked by many *professional* personnel people is: you, as the interviewer and as a representative of your company, must make a favorable enough impression on the candidate so that you won't have trouble hiring that individual should you wish to.

True, the purpose of an interview is to determine whether the candidate is suitable for a job. The better the candidate, however, the more likely it is that the person is also interviewing *you.*

I could cite any number of situations in which first and

even second hiring choices have been lost simply because the people doing the interviewing weren't sensitive enough to the importance of impressing the candidate. I can remember one company in particular in which a candidate for a VP of finance job called me to tell me that he'd had a miserable initial interview experience with an insolent assistant in the personnel department and that he had no intention of going back to the company for subsequent interviews. Fortunately, I was able to persuade this person not to judge a company by one employee. Five years later the candidate became the president of that company.

Avoiding the Most Common Pitfalls

Successful interviewing (in addition to following the two principles I've just discussed) is largely a matter of avoiding certain pitfalls—pitfalls that are so prevalent, you would almost think they were inherent in the process.

One pitfall is the tendency to prejudge candidates on the basis of résumés or recommendations. Another is to let these prejudgments prejudice the way you conduct the interview. When you fall victim to these tendencies, you interview not so much with the idea of eliciting information as to seek only that information that will affirm judgments you've already made.

Unfortunately, there is nothing specific I can suggest to prevent these all-too-common tendencies, other than to urge you to become more sensitive to how much they may be influencing your own strategy. Early on in my career, for instance, I trained myself to temper my enthusiasm for any candidate whose résumé or whose initial appearance made an unusually strong positive impression on me. It's not that I don't put any stock in first impressions or that I was frequently wrong about candidates who made good first impressions. It's more that I didn't want to hire the candidate before the interview.

This tendency can work the other way, too. You can draw so negative an impression from one aspect of a candidate's background that you become all but blind to the positive attributes in the candidate. In either case, it's a trap you must avoid if you're going to be successful at interviewing.

Keys to Successful Interviewing

Below are fifteen specifics necessary for a successful interview:

1. Screen carefully.
2. Have a plan.
3. Follow a logical sequence.

4. Create a proper interview environment.
5. Put the candidate at ease.
6. Let the candidate do the talking.
7. Perfect your questioning techniques.
8. Become a better listener.
9. Keep your reactions to yourself.
10. Stay in control.
11. Take notes.
12. Don't oversell the position.
13. Conclude the interview on the proper note.
14. Write an interview summary.
15. Learn from each experience.

1. Screen Carefully

Good screening procedures will go a long way to ensure that only candidates who have a reasonable chance of being hired are eventually interviewed. At the same time, however, you can't be so rigid in your screening procedures that you eliminate good candidates from consideration. In the long run, it's better to spend a little extra time interviewing a candidate who possibly didn't warrant an interview than to *not* get a look at somebody who deserved an interview but was screened out of the process by somebody's arbitrary decision.

The basic screening device in many situations will be

the information contained in the application form or the résumé. But should you come across a candidate whose résumé is not strong but who has written a compelling letter or comes with a recommendation from somebody you trust, that candidate is probably worth at least a phone call.

Talking to candidates by phone, by the way, is an excellent way to narrow down a large field. Try to turn such phone conversations into mini-interviews, in which you can single out those who appear to be worth a closer look. It's also a good idea to have a "borderline" candidate you talk to write you a letter detailing his or her strengths.

The phone interview is also useful before you go to the trouble or expense of bringing in a candidate from out of town.

2. Have a Plan

Although all employment interviews have the same basic objective—to draw enough information from the candidate so that you can make the proper hiring decision—you still need to spend a few moments before each interview to review in your own mind what you want to accomplish in that interview.

Not everyone agrees on how you should prepare. Some people feel so strongly about having an "open mind" when meeting a candidate for the first time, they caution you against even looking too carefully at the résumé.

I don't agree. You need to be familiar with the candidate's application form and résumé in order not to waste time getting information that's already available to you. I believe the best time to read the résumé, if you were not the first one to select it, is ten minutes before the interview. That way, the information is fresh in your mind. Be sure to pinpoint specific aspects of the résumé that you intend to address directly. The number of questions you can ask a candidate is enormous, and for this reason, you must tailor your questions to each candidate.

If you're not an experienced interviewer, you should jot down a general plan for the interview, along with certain specific questions you want to have answered. There's no need to memorize the questions.

The point is to be able to control the flow of the interview. You don't want to spend so much time on one particular aspect of the candidate's background that you don't have time to get to other important information.

3. Follow a Logical Sequence

The interview should always follow a logical sequence, although that sequence may not be the same for every interview. As a general rule, it's good to have candidates talk about their most recent job experience near the beginning of the interview.

It can be a good practice to talk, near the beginning of the interview, about the more concrete aspects of the candidate's background—what he or she actually did in the last job—and gradually move into specific qualities that make that candidate special.

All things considered, the following sequence will probably serve you well in most situations.

A. Greeting the candidate.
B. Putting the candidate at ease with brief small talk.
C. Giving an overview of what you want to accomplish in the interview.
D. Eliciting information about the candidate.
E. Describing the job.
F. Answering questions.
G. Closing the interview.

A couple of points deserve some elaboration here, if only because they're often overlooked.

Many interviewers, for instance, fail to give an overview. They fail to tell the candidate what the interview is meant to accomplish. Even though it's obvious, you should state why the candidate is here ("As you know, we're interviewing right now for a new vice-president of marketing") and give some indication as to what sort of information you're looking for ("What I want to gain from this interview is a general sense of your experience, your background, and some of the strengths you think you could bring to this position").

Whatever you choose to say in your opening remarks beyond this brief statement of objectives is up to you. There is no need at this point in the interview to tell the candidate what qualities the job demands, and it isn't necessary to remind candidates that they are one of dozens of people you're considering. Neither piece of information accomplishes anything.

You'll notice that I recommend that you not describe the job until *after* you elicit information from the candidate. It's a tactical mistake in the early stages of the interview to reveal details about the position, beyond a general job description. The more *you* talk about the job, the less time is left for the candidate to speak. But a more strategic reason for keeping this information to yourself is that you don't want to reveal too much to the candidate. If early in the interview you say, "We're looking for somebody who is extremely well-organized and detail-minded," a shrewd candidate will answer subsequent questions in a way calculated to give you the impression that he or she has those very qualities, whether they exist or not.

Exactly how much time you should allot for each interview is difficult to say. Most personnel professionals figure you need at least an hour for most job openings, but the actual amount of time you spend should depend more on the quality of the candidate. If it is patently clear after the first fifteen minutes or so of the interview that the candidate is unsuitable, it's a waste of time to go through the motions.

You have two options here. If the unsuitability is obvious to the two of you, there's nothing wrong with ending the interview (tactfully, of course) after the first fifteen minutes. If the decision is more yours—that is, you are convinced that this candidate is not right for the job but the candidate may not realize this—you can speed up the rest of the interview. Just be careful you don't indicate to the candidate that you've already made up your mind. Even those you don't hire should at least have the feeling that they've been given a reasonable chance to present their case.

Under normal circumstances, most of the interview will be taken up by step D (eliciting information about the candidate), in which you are asking the person specific questions. But don't allow this stage of the interview to run too long. Always allow time to cover the remaining steps, and do your best to end the interview on a fairly relaxed note.

4. Create a Proper Interview Environment

Hold the interview someplace where you won't be subjected to frequent interruptions. Interruptions are not only rude to the candidate, they disrupt the flow of the interview and make it that much more difficult for you to elicit and evaluate the information you're seeking. Little wonder that 95 percent of the respondents in our Burke survey agreed that you should do whatever you can to avoid interruptions during the job interview.

Your own office is probably the best place to conduct the interview, but if your office doesn't have a door (or has walls so thin you can hear what's going on in adjacent offices), find a more private, more quiet place.

To ensure that you don't get interrupted, have all calls intercepted and take whatever measures are necessary—a "do not disturb" sign, if need be—to keep visitors away. If your job is such that it's next to impossible to avoid interruptions, conduct the interview either before or after normal working hours, or arrange to hold the interview someplace outside your building: your recruiter's office, your accountant's office, your lawyer's office, or at your ad agency.

One element of the interview environment sometimes overlooked by interviewers is the number of people doing the interview. Once in a while it may be necessary for more than one person to be present during an interview, but avoid this practice whenever you can. I've heard of situations in which a candidate was interviewed by a dozen people at once (one candidate described such an encounter as one of the "most horrible experiences of my business career"). And I know of one company that likes to have a subordinate—somebody who might end up working for the candidate—present at the interview. Avoid both practices. They're inappropriate and counterproductive.

5. Put the Candidate at Ease

Being interviewed for a job is stressful for most people, but that stress is as much your problem as it is the candidate's. It's your responsibility, as the interviewer, to do whatever you can to ease the tension and establish a comfortable rapport.

There are two good reasons for making this effort. First, it's tough to generate a useful flow of information from candidates who are excessively nervous or uncomfortable. Unless you can get him or her to relax, you'll never get an accurate picture of the candidate, and you'll have all the more trouble trying to make a reasonably accurate assessment of the candidate's strengths and weaknesses.

Second, if the interview experience turns out to be particularly unpleasant and the candidate turns out to be the best person for the job, you could have trouble convincing the person to accept the job.

Remember, it's easy to forget that at the same time you're interviewing the candidate, the candidate is interviewing you—deciding whether or not your company or department is a good place to work.

Your concern for the candidate's state of mind during the interview should begin even before you meet. If the applicant will be greeted by a receptionist and secretary, let them know the candidate is coming, and remind each to greet the person warmly. (The person should never have to be asked, "Do you have an appointment?" but should be told, nicely, "We've been expecting you.")

87

It goes without saying that you should do your best to start the interview on time. Should you find yourself running late, make sure you inform the candidate—preferably in person—that you've been detained and give an estimate of how long the wait is likely to be.

One thing you can do at the start to put the candidate at ease is to greet the person in the waiting room. Introduce yourself and then accompany the applicant into the office where the two of you are going to sit down and talk. Taking the initiative in this manner eliminates the awkwardness that most people feel whenever they walk into an unfamiliar setting to find somebody simply *waiting* there behind a desk.

Be courteous. Keep in mind that the candidate is likely to be hypersensitive to any sign that you're preoccupied or harried. Do whatever you can to make the candidate feel genuinely welcome (offering coffee, tea, or a soft drink, for instance).

It's essential, too—even if you're a little pressed for time—to start off the interview with some very brief small talk: about the weather, about the construction that may be going on outside the office, about *anything* that isn't going to be threatening to the candidate. Your objective here is to relax the person you're interviewing. And make sure that during the interview you give the candidate your undivided attention. Concentrate on the person, not on the papers on your desk, and not on what might be going on outside your window.

One final suggestion concerning the arrangement of the room: I've always preferred a coffee-table type of setting when I'm interviewing. I find that candidates are usually more relaxed in this kind of setting than they would be across a desk.

6. Let the Candidate Do the Talking

One of the biggest mistakes inexperienced interviewers make is to do too much of the talking. The general rule of thumb: when you're interviewing a job candidate, you, the interviewer, should do no more than 30 percent of the talking.

Apart from conveying basic information about the job, everything you say should be directed toward getting the candidate to talk. Resist the temptation to share opinions with the candidate on issues that have no relevance to the job, and keep whatever comments and observations you may want to make about the candidate's responses as brief as possible.

Bear in mind, too, that experienced job seekers will do their best to get you to do more of the talking, so that they can get a better sense of what you're looking for and tailor their answers accordingly. If you run into a candidate who persists in asking too many questions, and appears to be controlling the interview, the best thing to do is to inform the candidate politely that you'll answer questions at the end of the interview but that you have some important information to gather first.

7. Perfect Your Questioning Techniques

Knowing *how* to ask questions when you're interviewing a candidate is just as important as knowing which questions to ask.

There are several different ways of asking the same question, and depending on the situation you may want to vary the approach. Here are some options:

• **Closed-ended.** Closed-ended questions require a "yes" or "no" answer. ("Do you enjoy supervising people?") They're fine for simple factual matters ("Did you earn a commission in your last job?"), but they should be used sparingly because they don't encourage the candidate to talk.

• **Open-ended.** Open-ended questions force the candidate to elaborate on a response. ("What are your feelings about supervising people?") This is the form that most of your questions should take, and this is the form of questioning preferred by the vast majority of our Burke survey respondents.

• **Leading.** Leading questions are those in which you indicate the response you would like to hear. ("What is it about supervising people you like—the challenge of it?") It's generally a good practice to *avoid* such questions unless you have a specific purpose in mind, such as when the answer you're fishing for is *not* really the best response to the question. I do not like this practice, but some interviewers trying to ascertain whether a candidate is a team player or not will ask, "You don't think it's important to always go through channels, do you?"

• **Hypothetical.** Hypothetical questions are questions in which you set up a "what if" situation. ("What if I asked you to supervise the staff?") Such questions, if strategically asked, can give you insight into how the candidate thinks.

• **Loaded.** Loaded questions are questions in which you ask the candidate to choose the lesser of two evils. "Do you enjoy firing people or do you consider yourself a softie?" would be an exaggerated version of such a question. Such questions should be avoided.

• **Multiple.** A multiple question, as the name implies, is several questions at once. ("Tell me about your last supervisor. What were her strengths and her weaknesses? What do you think you learned from her?") The problem with multiple questions is that you can rarely expect to get satisfactory answers to all of them at once. Frequently, the candidate will forget the first stage of the question before you've had a chance to finish asking the second stage.

Apart from the way you phrase questions, give thought to how you organize and pace your questions. Remember

91

that if you're running an interview properly, the result will be a *conversation*, not a grilling session.

Whenever possible, try to phrase your questions indirectly and offhandedly. "What would you say, if you had to think about it, were your greatest strengths?" is better than a flat "What are your strengths?"

Make sure, too, you give the candidate plenty of time to answer each question. Don't feel obliged to throw another question at the candidate as soon as the last one has been answered. Pause a few seconds to think about each response (as well as to make sure the candidate doesn't want to say more on the topic). Do your best to link new questions to the past answer. ("Fine, so we've established that you enjoy taking on responsibility—let's talk a little about how you like to supervise.")

You shouldn't hesitate to probe—that is, seek more detailed or more elaborate answers to a question—but try not to probe in a threatening manner, you don't want to put the candidate on the defensive. "That's interesting—could you tell me more about that?" is better than "What do you mean by *that?*" "Maybe you could clarify that point a little for me" is better than a curt "Why?"

Finally, try to balance your questions so that you're not emphasizing the negatives too much. Should you find a candidate who is hesitant to talk about a subject, don't force the issue unless it's a critical area relating directly to the job. Forcing the issue early in the interview will only put the candidate on guard and make it that much tougher for you to get candid answers later on.

8. Become a Better Listener

To interview effectively, you must be able to *listen* effectively. This means that you must do more than simply "hear" the responses; you need to actively focus on these responses and, just as important, give the candidate enough feedback to encourage more in-depth answers.

We all know how inhibiting and irritating it can be to sense that everything we're saying is simply going over the head of the person who is supposed to be listening. Unfortunately, however, listening is *not* something that comes naturally to most people, particularly in an interview situation. Because there are usually many questions you want to have answered and you're interested in the answers to these questions, there's a natural tendency to look ahead at what you *intend* to ask, or look back to reflect on a previous answer.

You need to fight the tendency. When you're interviewing someone, you must discipline yourself to focus not only on *what* is being said but on *how* it's being said.

If you do this—if you truly concentrate on what's being said—the other listening "skills" come more or less naturally. Yes, it's important, as most people stress, that you respond actively to what is being said, whether by a statement of agreement, a nod of the head, or a change of expression. But I've discovered that if I'm truly listening—that is, truly focusing on what the person is saying—I don't

93

have to think about all the various mechanics of listening. They simply happen. There is one specific skill related to listening, however, that deserves special mention: the use of silence.

Silence can be awkward in any situation, the job interview being no exception. But don't feel compelled to talk simply because there is a moment of silence. Pauses give you time to reflect on an answer and to decide whether you want to pursue something further. Experienced interviewers, in fact, often use silence to good advantage. By nodding silently and maintaining eye contact, you indicate to the candidate that you're waiting for a point to be clarified or elaborated upon.

9. Keep Your Reactions to Yourself

Do your best—apart from the responses you give to keep the candidate talking—to keep any emotional reactions to what the candidate is saying during the interview to yourself. The job interview—particularly the initial interview—is not the place in which to challenge points raised by the candidate.

The reason it's so important to keep your judgments to yourself is that astute candidates will be sensitive to nonvocal indications—your body language, your facial expression, etc.—and may use these cues for feedback and adjust their answers accordingly.

10. Stay in Control

It's easier than you might imagine to lose control of an interview, particularly with a candidate who has a good deal of experience in job interviews.

Some candidates, as I indicated earlier, will do their best to get you talking, while others will try to steer the interview away from areas they'd rather not talk about in favor of those areas that showcase their strengths. Your task in these situations is very simple: you have to shift the focus away from you and toward the candidate, and you have to steer the candidate (firmly but tactfully) to the areas that you want to explore.

There is no single technique for staying in control of an interview. It's primarily a matter of knowing ahead of time what you're looking for and being alert during the interview to signs that you're moving off course.

11. Take Notes

Some people consider it rude and inhibiting to the candidate if you take notes, and you are often advised against doing it.

I don't agree. If you don't take notes, you're likely to forget most of the details of the interview. Worse, you're likely to remember only those details that you *want* to remember. Then, when the time comes to evaluate the candidate, you'll rely on your overall or "gut" reaction to the candidate. You'll also give less consideration to candidates interviewed early on, not because they aren't qualified but because you've forgotten some of their essential facts.

Naturally, you shouldn't attempt to record *everything* that is said, and you should do your best to underplay the note taking. Even as you're writing, for instance, you should try to maintain some eye contact. You don't want the candidates to become so aware of the notes you're taking that they deliberately slow down their answers.

12. Don't Oversell the Position

Regardless of how much a candidate impresses you during the interview, resist the temptation to oversell the position. Your objective when you're filling a position, remember, is not simply to hire someone, it's to make sure the person you hire represents a good "fit" with the job and will be with you for many years to come.

Be as factual as you can when you are describing the position, particularly with respect to the negatives (travel, night or weekend work). It might interest you to know that

Xerox Corporation has candidates for sales jobs view a film that emphasizes all of the difficulties of selling. Their rationale: they want to weed out the candidates who will throw in the towel as soon as the going gets a little tough.

Be frank about salary and career potential, but avoid lengthy discussions on either topic, particularly on salary. Candidates have a right to know what the job pays, but the initial interview is not—repeat, not—the place to negotiate salary. The only time to negotiate salary is when you are likely to make a job offer. If a candidate tells you point-blank that he or she wants more money than the job pays (generally a mistake on the candidate's part, in my view), you have to use your judgment. If this person is a top contender, don't close the door. Say you'll give the matter some thought, that you'll talk to others in the company and report back. Later, you may decide that you don't want to pay that high a salary. In the meantime, the candidate might have a change of heart and accept your offer.

13. Conclude the Interview on the Proper Note

The best way to end the interview will depend, in part, on your impression of the candidate during the interview. But certain principles apply to all interviews.

It's up to you to let the candidate know that the inter-

97

view is about to end. You can give this indication in several ways: by closing your notebook, or removing your glasses, or simply by announcing, "This will be my last question," or "We only have a couple more minutes, is there anything else you want to discuss?" You should then stand up, thank the person for coming in, and walk the candidate to the door.

That's the etiquette aspect of ending the interview. What you actually say to the candidate should depend on what your next step in the process is likely to be. Here are the options:

• **Definite "nos."** With candidates you know for certain you're not going to hire, thank them for their time and tell them that you're interviewing a number of people and you will notify them if you want them to come back for a second interview. If you don't intend to notify them formally, tell them that if they don't hear from you within a certain period (a week, perhaps), they can assume that you've hired somebody else.

• **Possibles.** When candidates look promising, I see nothing wrong with expressing interest, so long as you don't commit yourself. Tell the candidate that you will be in touch within a certain period of time and make sure you are, whether or not you choose that person.

• **Top contenders.** I've known managers who've been so impressed with a candidate after the first interview, and so concerned that they might lose the candidate, that they've offered the job right on the spot. I admire decisiveness, but I don't recommend this kind of decisiveness except under three unusual conditions: (1) you've been looking for a long time to fill a specialized position and you're positive you've found the right person; (2) the person has a background that is extremely hard to find; or (3) the person is unemployed and you're prepared to offer a trial period (with no commitments) of a week or so.

The reason I urge you not to move so quickly is to guard against one of the tendencies we'll examine more closely later: namely, that you become so infatuated with a candidate during the interview that you lose your objectivity and become blind to faults that begin to surface as soon as the person becomes an employee.

If you're very high on the applicant, you can say so, but ask for a day or two to make up your mind. It's rare that an applicant will be in such demand that you'll lose the person if you don't make the offer at that very moment. So there's no need to panic.

On the other hand, don't stall unnecessarily when you find someone you want to hire. I can't tell you how many times companies have lost excellent people because they waited too long to send a letter of acceptance. In the meantime, the candidate took another job.

One more thing. I believe you should do your best to notify the people you interviewed who were not hired. (I prefer writing, but a telephone call is all right too.) Let them know that you've hired someone else. Here's a sample of the kind of note you might send.

Dana Fitch
234 W. Elm
Anywhere, U.S.A.

Dear Ms. Fitch:

I'm writing to thank you for taking the time recently to discuss the position [name the position] and to tell you, regretfully, that although I was impressed with your background, we've found someone who seems to be a better fit for the job.

Be assured I will keep your résumé and application on file and will contact you should there be an opening that might be better suited for you.

Best of luck.

Jean Dailey
Vice-President

Such a note not only takes the edge off the rejection, it is excellent public relations for your company.

14. Write an Interview Summary

As soon as possible after each interview ends, while the information is still fresh in your mind, write—or dictate into a tape recorder—a brief evaluation of the candidate you've just interviewed. Don't worry about objectivity at this point. Simply record some of your impressions—what struck you as the candidate's strengths and weaknesses.

In addition to giving you some additional feedback that will be important when the time comes to compare candidates, writing down your impressions does something else as well: once you've done some thinking about all the various people you've seen, you have a chance to measure the accuracy of your initial impressions. The H-I-R-E form on pages 168–169 can be an excellent tool for this evaluation.

15. Learn from Each Experience

After each interview (or after each day of interviewing), it's always a good idea to review how you handled yourself. Here's a checklist of some of the questions you might consider:

Were you able to prevent interruptions?
Did you take special efforts to put the candidate at ease?
Did you obtain the information you wanted to get from the candidate?
Did you probe deeply enough into important areas?
Did you concentrate on listening?
Did you stay in control of the interview?
Did you end on the appropriate note?

Will the notes you took be helpful?
Were you objective in describing the position?
What specific aspect of the interview do you think you might handle better the next time?

7 | ON WHAT QUESTIONS TO ASK IN THE INTERVIEW

Asking the right questions takes as much skill as giving the right answers.

Let's begin with the questions you *shouldn't* ask—questions, that is, that could get you into hot water with the Equal Employment Opportunity Commission.

You are breaking a federal law (and often a state law as well) by asking any questions directly or indirectly relating to the following aspects of the candidate's background:

- Religion
- Race or color
- National origin
- Age
- Sex
- Marital or family status
- Handicaps
- Criminal record
- Financial affairs

Let's look more closely at each of these areas.

Race or Color

Discriminatory questions involving race or color are fairly easy to avoid. Here too, you need to be careful about *indirect* references to race or color in your questions. To ask a white candidate if he or she would be "comfortable" working in a black neighborhood, or a black candidate if he or she would be "comfortable" working in a white neighborhood, is discriminatory, as are any questions aimed at finding out a candidate's personal views on race. Race, it goes without saying, should *never* be a factor in a hiring decision, so keep any reference to it out of the interview.

Religion

Never ask *any* questions that relate to a candidate's religious background, beliefs, or practices. In particular, never make the mistake of asking a candidate to give you the origin of his or her last name, and ask no questions about social affiliations (such as college fraternity or sorority) that could yield information about a candidate's religion.

In rare situations, of course, this prohibition could cause a problem. If the job calls for Sunday or Saturday work and the candidate goes to religious services on either day, the candidate is probably not the best choice. So, while a question like "Will you be able to work on Saturdays?" is legitimate, you need to be able to show that Saturday work is a bona fide job requirement. The safest route in this instance is to simply list that job requirement along with all the others and then ask the candidate if there are any aspects of the job that, for any reason, he or she might not be able to handle.

Incidentally, if candidates themselves bring up the issue of religious beliefs, it's up to you to end the subject. Say to the candidate, "Your religious beliefs really don't have any bearing on this job," or "Let's go on to another subject." If the candidate persists, explain the law and reiterate your intention *not* to talk about religion.

Never forget the principle: if you simply eliminate any question or conversation having to do with religion, you avoid trouble.

National Origin

Everything I've said thus far about a candidate's religion and race or color applies as well to a candidate's national origin. You *are* permitted to ask if a candidate is a U.S. citizen. And if language skills are related to the job, you can ask candidates what languages they speak fluently, just so long as you steer away from questions aimed at *how* candidates may have learned the language. You *can't* ask candidates to tell you where they, their parents, or their spouses were born, and you can't ask for names of clubs or societies that might reveal religion or national origin.

Age

Since it is illegal to discriminate on the basis of age (the federal law specifically protects people between the ages of forty and seventy), you're not permitted to ask any questions that might reveal to you how old the candidate is. Strictly speaking, you are not allowed to ask if a candidate was a veteran of a specific war. Neither can you ask how old a candidate's children are. Also to be avoided are questions that indirectly relate to age, such as "How would you feel working in an environment in which everyone is younger than you?"

Sex and Marital or Family Status

Most of the laws regarding discrimination on the basis of sex have been designed to give women the same rights as men when applying for jobs. So the rule here is very simple: don't ask a woman anything you wouldn't ask a man. And vice versa.

You can't ask either men or women any questions about their domestic life: whether they're married or not, the number of children they have (or the ages of those children), or even the occupation of their spouses. Even a question like "How do you think your family will react to all the travel you might have to do in this job?" is discriminatory. Instead, you need to phrase the same question as follows: "How much time will you be able to spend traveling on this job?"

Handicaps

The general rule of thumb regarding the hiring of anybody with a physical handicap is that you can't eliminate a handicapped person from consideration unless the person's handicap will *measurably* and directly affect job performance. What's more, questions regarding height and weight are almost invariably discriminatory except in those rare situations in which the job truly requires people within a specific height range.

Criminal Record

People who've been convicted of crimes are not protected by legislation as much as other groups, but you need to be careful how you phrase any questions about their criminal record. You *can't* ask candidates to tell if they've ever been arrested, but you *can* ask them if they have ever been *convicted* of a crime, and you're permitted to—and indeed should—probe for details.

Financial Affairs

Although you are permitted (in most states) to run a standard credit check on a candidate, most questions regarding financial affairs are illegal. You can't ask candidates whether they own their own home or car, or how much money they owe.

Playing It Safe

If I seem overly sensitive about these issues, it's for a good reason: whatever information you're likely to get when you ask questions that could be interpreted as discriminatory could never be worth the grief you're likely to bring upon yourself and your company should a candidate choose to complain.

This caveat, incidentally, applies to areas in addition to those I've already mentioned. Certain questions relating to a candidate's personal habits and attitudes *could* leave you open to charges of sexual harassment, regardless of how innocent those questions may be. Indeed, you need to be careful that *nothing* you say or do during the interview carries even the slightest hint of a sexual overture.

So what *can* you ask? Questions that relate specifically to the candidate's prior educational and work experience and to any of the candidate's attitudes that have an obvious bearing on the job.

Questions that fall within this framework can be arranged in any number of ways. I've chosen the following categories:

- Work history
- Job-related skills and knowledge
- General intelligence and aptitude
- Attitudes and personality
- Education

I've listed some recommended questions for each of these categories, but let's first look at what your objective should be whenever you're questioning the candidate in each of these areas.

Work History

Questions relating to candidates' work history should go beyond a simple description of their jobs. These questions should delve into such areas as level of responsibility, accomplishments, earnings, and how their work related to others'.

With some candidates (assuming there's time) it's best to go through the entire work history, making sure, however, that you don't spend too much time on any single area and that the candidate can account for all gaps in time between jobs. If you're interviewing a candidate with a wealth of experience, you're probably better off skimming over the early jobs and concentrating on the most recent work experiences.

Job-Related Skills and Knowledge

Questions relating to the candidate's skills and knowledge differ from questions about work history in that here you're trying to find out *exactly* what the candidate *did* on the job: what a typical day was like, what kinds of activities took up most of the candidate's time, the kind of decisions he or she had to make, and so forth.

What you're looking for in this category of questions are specifics. Don't assume that simply because candidates had a certain title, they had full responsibility for the jobs normally associated with that title. Being a "director of marketing" in one firm may mean something quite different from being a "director of marketing" in *your* firm. Don't be afraid to probe: if candidates say they were "responsible" for something, find out exactly what they mean by "responsible."

It's also important to find out what the candidate's boss and colleagues did. That way you can gauge how much the person you're interviewing was actually responsible for the work that got done.

110

General Intelligence and Aptitude

You can frequently get a fair idea of candidates' general intelligence and aptitude from the way they answer questions, but you should still ask a few questions related directly to these two qualities. Given two candidates similar in all other respects, the candidate who has the edge in intelligence and aptitude is usually the better choice, albeit with one exception: when a candidate is *too* intelligent for the job and an imminent promotion is unlikely.

A word of warning: be careful, as I suggested in the previous chapter, about judging intelligence on the basis of appearance. One of the biggest mistakes you can make as an interviewer is to make *any* assumptions about personality, character, or intelligence on the basis of appearance.

Attitudes and Personality

You can infer a great deal about the attitudes and personality of the candidates through the way they answer questions, but you should still ask questions designed to give you greater insight. Donald H. Trautlein, chairman of the Bethlehem Steel Corporation, for example, once told me that he has always focused on these two areas in the interviews he himself has conducted. "I'm mostly concerned," he said, "with the subjective judgment of the candidate, with the general matching of their chemistry to ours, and with shared values."

It's important that you get an idea of what tasks the candidates like or dislike doing, not only because people are invariably better at the things they like to do, but because people who *don't* like what they do rarely last long on the job. Better to find out during the interview than after you hire.

Education

Questions about education are important but should occupy only a relatively small portion of the interview and should be used primarily when there isn't job-related experience to discuss. Nonetheless, it's possible to gain valuable insight into a candidate on the basis of that candidate's academic performance and attitudes about education.

Good Questions to Ask

There are any number of questions you could ask during an interview. Clearly, you should choose those most likely to generate the most pertinent information possible. And select the questions prior to interviewing *each* candidate. Don't necessarily ask all of the same questions of everyone you interview for a given job. Some will have to be specially selected if you observe from the résumé that there may be a particular problem with that applicant.

Here are some examples of excellent questions that you can consider using.

Experience

What is your boss's title and what are your boss's functions?

This question should *always* be asked—and early in the interview. The answer will indicate how much work the candidate actually did, and discourages the person from exaggerating the importance of his or her functions.

Don't let the candidate skirt this question. If you're told the boss did little, make sure the candidate elaborates. It's unlikely, for instance, that the candidate did everything and the boss did nothing. I've often wondered how employers would react if they had a chance to see the résumé of a former employee, particularly an employee they were happy to see go. I've seen the résumés of such employees,

113

who worked for very successful companies, and wondered how their company was managing without them.

It's also useful to learn early on if candidates really don't know what their bosses did. Such ignorance indicates a lack of depth and interest in the company, and could explain why they're looking for another job.

Would you describe a typical day in your job for me?

Another question you should *always* ask, primarily because it forces the candidate to be specific and gives you a chance to see how closely the candidate's day-to-day duties relate to the day-to-day duties of the job you're looking to fill.

Tell me about the people you hired in your last job. How long did they stay with you, and how did they work out?

An excellent set of questions to ask somebody applying for a managerial position. The answers will give you an idea of the candidate's ability to assemble—and keep—a strong staff, and could reveal a personality problem (for example, the candidate has never been able to keep a secretary for more than a few months).

114

What do you consider the single most important idea you contributed or your single most noteworthy accomplishment in your present job?

This question is a good way to find out if the candidate is able to substantiate the details of an impressive résumé. Many résumés give a general impression of accomplishment, but when you ask a candidate to name *specific* contributions or ideas, you separate the winners from the rest of the pack.

An additional thought here: some candidates—you might call them "sleepers"—have contributed more ideas and accomplished more than even *they* are aware of. It's probably worth your while to see if you can coax answers out of an applicant who has trouble answering this question.

Specific Job Skills and Knowledge

How would you proceed to install a standard cost accounting system?

I've used this example from accounting to illustrate the point of this kind of question: to determine whether a candidate has the basic technical knowledge to fill the job.

115

You should always try to include at least one occupational question, simply to make sure that the candidate isn't trying to bluff. The reason: many job seekers are experts at getting jobs but lack the skills to carry them out. You don't necessarily have to be an expert in this field to judge whether the candidate really knows the technical requirements. Trust your judgment. If you have doubts, ask others in the company to quiz the candidate on the specifics.

What do you think it takes for a person to be successful in [fill in the particular specialty]?

This question represents an indirect but often effective way of having candidates reveal their own strengths and weaknesses. Most people, when answering this question, will answer it within the context of their own strengths and weaknesses. When they're talking about what it takes to succeed, they'll name what they perceive to be their own strengths.

If you ran into this situation [give a typical problem situation the candidate might be expected to deal with as an employee], how would you handle it?

I'm not overly fond of hypothetical questions (I prefer questions that reveal what the candidate has actually *done* and not what the candidate *might* do), but this question is an exception. The more specific you can be when you ask this question—that is, the more the question relates to specific technical requirements or knowledge—the more valuable the answer will be to you.

What specific strengths did you bring to your last job that made you effective?

I like this question because it covers a lot of territory and gives you a good chance to compare the answers the candidate gives to the answers regarding what the candidate's boss did. If the candidate did, in fact, have the responsibility indicated by the earlier answer, he or she should be able to explain the strengths that underlie the performance.

What specific strengths do you think you can bring to this position?

I prefer to use this question on candidates who've come back for a second interview. The problem with asking it in the initial interview is that you may not have spelled out what the job is, so the candidate has no way of answering it.

If you've already spelled out the needs of the job, be wary of the response. A shrewd candidate might tailor answers accordingly. Probe more deeply for specific *illustrations* of strengths.

117

General Intelligence and Aptitude

Can you tell me a little bit about how you go about making important decisions?

This is a rarely asked key question that can give you a sense of how the candidate is likely to operate on the job. Be sensitive to how much—or how little—the candidate likes to seek out others for advice or information. See if you can figure out from the response if the candidate is action-oriented or analytical, and make a mental note of whether that style of decision making is what you need in your company or department.

Beware of pat answers—answers that indicate a rigid "by the numbers" approach to decision making. The best decision makers in business are people who tailor their decision making to each individual situation. Indeed, this ability to vary strategy is one of the most reliable measures of managerial effectiveness.

What are some of the things your company might have done to be more successful?

Candidates who can give you a perceptive answer to this question are giving you fairly concrete evidence that they are aware of the "big picture." Candidates who can't answer it at all are usually revealing a lack of depth. Sometimes, too, this question can elicit the "sour grapes" that they may be harboring but are doing their best to keep from you. A candidate who says something like "Well, they didn't use me well . . ." could be revealing a personality problem. Usually, when a company doesn't use an employee well, there's a good reason.

What do you know about our company?

What you're trying to find out in this question is how much time (if any) the candidate has spent learning about your company and how resourceful the candidate has been in getting that information. If candidates can't tell you much about your company, they should at least indicate that they made an effort to obtain some information. I'm not saying you should rule out candidates who *haven't* researched your company—only that you give due credit to the candidates who have done so.

Attitudes and Personality

Could you tell me why you're interested in this job?

Your objective in this frequently asked question is to separate the candidates who just want a job—any job—from those who are genuinely interested in your company and in the job you want to fill. The question can also help you to identify the candidates whose career ambitions are consistent with the opportunities of the job. Look for evidence that the individual has done homework on your company, and look, too, for the ability to communicate to you what *specific* contributions he or she can make.

Why have you decided to leave your present position?

Taken at face value, this question can often reveal what truly motivates a candidate: money, career growth, or personal challenge. The problem, though, is that many of the "employed" candidates you interview will, in fact, have been fired from their previous job but given time to find a new position. Candidates who fall into this category shouldn't be eliminated, but if they were fired, you'll want to know why.

What would you like to be earning two years from now?

A question that gives you a general sense of the candidate's career goals, tells you if those career goals are likely to be met in your company, and helps you judge whether the employee has a realistic sense of his or her own worth in the marketplace.

120

What do you consider your most significant accomplishments in your business life?

This question forces candidates to substantiate the strengths they claim to have. Ask it in every interview where the applicant has substantial experience.

What have been the biggest failures or frustrations in your business life?

The answer will often reflect how well they know themselves and how comfortable they are about revealing their weaknesses. Be alert, however, for experienced candidates who are shrewd enough to reveal "weaknesses" that could be interpreted as strengths (for example, "I expect too much from myself"). Press for details.

What risks did you take in your last few jobs, and what was the result of those risks?

This is a rarely asked question, but it can separate outstanding managerial candidates from run-of-the-mill applicants. The reason: more and more studies of highly successful people reveal that on the average they are more likely to take calculated risks than people who are less successful. If a candidate can't mention any specific risks, go on to the next question. If the candidate can talk about risks, find out the rationale behind the risk (this will give some insight into the candidate's judgment) and what the results were.

Think about something you consider a failure in your life, and tell me why you think it occurred.

What you're looking for here are signs that a candidate is willing to accept responsibility for something that went wrong, but don't be quick to make assumptions. Astute candidates understand that most interviewers are wary of people who blame others for their shortcomings. Don't be afraid to probe more deeply. If candidates can't give you specific reasons *why* the failure was "their" fault, they may not really believe what they're telling you.

How did you enjoy working for your former employer?

This question can sometimes unmask malcontents: people who have a history of not being able to get along with employers. You're not necessarily looking for a candidate to rhapsodize about his or her former employers, but you want to be wary of anybody whose criticism is excessive. Someday the candidate could be saying similar things about you.

What do you do when you're having trouble solving a problem?

The answer here could indicate the presence—or absence—of a number of qualities and should also tell you a little of how dependent, or independent, the candidate is likely to be when in need of assistance. If you're the kind of supervisor who doesn't like to get directly involved in improving the work performance of your employees, you'll want to think twice about hiring someone who relied too heavily on his or her former boss for help.

What did you do in your last job to make yourself more effective?

The more specific you can get the candidate to be when answering this question, the better. If a candidate mentions graduate course work, as an example, look for some correlation between the schoolwork and the benefits or potential benefits to the job.

Where do you see yourself three years down the road?

You can get a general idea here (assuming the candidate is telling you the truth) of how ambitious the candidate is and, based on other information you gain from the interview, whether these ambitions are realistic.

Tell me about your hobbies and interests.

What people choose to do when they're not working can often give you a better glimpse of who they are as a person than you can get from their job performance.

What's the most monotonous job you ever had?

I prefer this question to the more familiar "What tasks do you find boring?" because the answer tells you more about the candidate. A candidate who has been *successful* at a job with a great deal of monotony (and most jobs have some monotony attached to them) indicates the ability to cope with the monotonous parts of work.

Describe the best boss you ever had.

The answer to this question usually indicates what kind of supervision the candidate likes—whether the candidate likes to work closely with a supervisor or prefers to be left alone. It also suggests how receptive the candidate is likely to be to criticism.

What kind of references do you think your previous employers will give you?

This question should be coupled with an assurance that you won't call without the candidate's permission. Those who have trouble answering this question are revealing one of two things, neither of which is particularly positive. First, they may be hiding something about their background. But barring deception, candidates who have little idea of how they were perceived by their former employers may be telling you they're not sure themselves of how well they performed in their last job.

Keep in mind, of course, that the reference information you eventually get might have been prearranged: that is, the candidate and the employer may have already agreed as to what the reference will be. It's wise to contact references at the candidate's former company that the candidate did not suggest you contact.

Education

Why did you decide (or not decide) to go to college?

This question can sometimes be a good way to determine how goal-oriented a candidate is and can give you some insight into how long the person has been interested in the field related to the position.

If the applicant's major in college was unrelated to the present occupational goals, find out the reason for pursuing that curriculum in the first place.

125

Tell me a little about how well you did in school.

While a candidate's academic record may not have too much bearing on the job at hand, there are good reasons to examine it. Academic performance is at least a partial indicator of intelligence, and can also reflect discipline and work habits. Candidates who appear to be unusually intelligent but earned only average grades in school could well have a low boredom threshold, which would make them unsuitable for many kinds of jobs. Candidates who did exceptionally well with what appears to be only average intelligence are often individuals with a strong sense of determination.

When you come across candidates who started but didn't complete college, find out why. Often the reason will be logical and justifiable (financial circumstances, for instance), but if the candidate flunked out of school, was suspended, or simply got bored and dropped out, you'll want to know it.

What were your best and worst subjects?

What you're looking here for are signs that relate to the technical requirements of the job. What I was always on the lookout for when I asked this question were those rare candidates who showed strengths in several areas. One of the strongest candidates I ever interviewed—who has gone on to become a highly successful financial executive—was a young woman who not only had a straight-A average in all her accounting and financial courses but was also an editor on her college paper.

What sort of jobs did you have while you were at school?

You can generally assume that those who were able to hold down jobs and still maintain good grades can handle pressure. But you shouldn't hold it *against* a candidate because he or she didn't hold down a job while in college. It's generally a safe assumption that a college graduate who has been working for several years will have an easier time adjusting to the workplace than a graduate who has never worked.

Tell me a little about your extracurricular activities.

A candidate's extracurricular activities can be a more accurate reflection of his or her potential than grades alone. The important consideration is not so much the *number* of activities as the nature of the involvement. It's well established that leadership patterns begin to emerge early in a person's life. So it's worth finding out if the candidate simply belonged to an organization or held a leadership position.

127

SUGGESTIONS FROM THE PROS

Our Burke study sought to find some "favorite" question among the professionals queried. Here are some additional questions you might find useful.

•What did you do the day before yesterday—in detail?

•Why do you think we should hire you?

•What are the most difficult aspects of your current job, and how do you approach them?

•Where do you think the power comes from in your organization?

•Tell me three characteristics about yourself.

•What do you think might differentiate you from other applicants?

8 | ON "READING" THE CANDIDATE

The greatest strength of some job candidates is their ability to impress the people who interview them.

The more you can learn about those personality traits that relate directly to job performance, the better you'll be able to judge how qualified the candidate is for the job. But how much can you trust your assessment of the candidate's personality on the strength of one or two interviews?

It's not an easy question to answer. Most personnel professionals will tell you that trying to get an accurate reading of a candidate's personality in one (or even two or three) interviews is all but impossible—even for highly experienced interviewers. The problem, they point out, isn't only the limited amount of time you have to make the assessment. The personality that many candidates reveal during the interview may not be what you're likely to see once they're on the job.

There are other problems. Clever interviewees, for instance, know how to showcase their personality strengths and conceal their weaknesses. What's more, behavior can be interpreted in different ways. Candidates who seem unusually relaxed during interviews could be either extremely confident or simply indifferent. Candidates who seem unusually energetic during the interview might very well be nervous.

Yet, I'm convinced that the impression you get of the candidate's personality *should* figure strongly in the hiring decision, and I'm convinced, too, that you *can* draw useful impressions of candidates on the strength of a single interview—with three important qualifications:

1. That you recognize the obstacles you're up against when you try to assess a candidate's personality traits, and you limit the impressions you try to draw.
2. That you understand and hold in check your own prejudices and your own tendencies to make snap judgments.
3. That you always seek confirmation (through questioning and through references) of those impressions on which you intend to base your hiring decision.

What to Look For

It's rare that any *single* facet of a candidate's behavior during the interview will accurately reflect the whole personality. Rather, you should draw a collective impression from a variety of inputs:

130

• **Your general impression.** Your general impression of the candidate should be just that—how you react on a person-to-person level and how you feel, generally, about the way the candidate might work out in your company or department.

It's essential that this impression be viewed in its proper perspective. As I noted earlier, applicants rarely give a complete picture of themselves during an interview. At best, you're only getting an indication of what they're like.

You must also do your best to evaluate the impression within the context of the *job*. A winning personality, for example, is an asset to any candidate, but if the job doesn't really *require* a winning personality, don't give this quality more importance than it deserves.

Consider some of the answers in our Burke study when respondents were asked to name the most *unusual thing* that a candidate ever did at an interview:

• "Got angry and talked very badly about a previous employer."

• "Bounced up and down on my carpet and told me I was highly thought of by the company because I was given such thick carpet."

• "Asked me highly personal questions."

• "Tried to hit me."

- "Gave me a sermon on religion to convert me to his beliefs."

- "Brought a goatskin of wine and drank it."

- "Positioned his body at a 45-degree angle and looked at the wall when I was asking questions."

Fortunately, very few candidates go to these extremes.

- **Manner of answering questions.** Just as important as *what* candidates say in response to questions is *how* they phrase and pace their answers. Pay attention to whether the answers you're receiving are genuinely thoughtful or simply rehearsed responses likely to have been given at every interview. (Pat answers frequently indicate a lack of depth.) See how often the candidate rationalizes when discussing failures. Rationalizations often reveal a lack of confidence and maturity.

See if you can discern certain patterns. Be wary of candidates who are excessively dogmatic in their answers—or excessively equivocating. Either extreme could indicate a negative personality trait.

- **Body language.** Body language has to do with the physical mannerisms people unconsciously make when they are communicating in face-to-face situations: how they carry themselves when they walk into a room, the way they sit, what they do with their hands when they're speaking, whether or not they look directly at you when answering questions. Some students of body language will tell you that people who tend to lean forward when they're talking to you usually have more forceful personalities than those who drop their shoulders or cross their arms. And they claim that people who conspicuously avoid looking you in the eye when they speak to you could be low in self-esteem.

You have to be careful, of course, not to go overboard when you're interpreting body language. But body language could be a way of confirming or questioning other impressions during the interview. I was always sensitive, in particular, to inconsistencies between what the person was verbalizing and what that person was saying with body language.

How to Target Your Judgments

Don't even attempt a complete personality reading of any candidate you interview. Concentrate instead on two, or at the most three, specific characteristics—those characteristics that you have already determined are most directly related to job performance.

Industriousness

The vast majority of the respondents in our Burke study agreed that the best way to determine if candidates are hard workers is to examine their accomplishments, responsibilities, and work experience.

Intelligence

One of the most brilliant candidates I ever interviewed could do incredibly complicated mathematical calculations in his head, but was just about hopeless when it came to solving problems that called for simple, practical solutions. Intelligence is extremely difficult to measure. Even IQ tests don't really reflect the ability to use native intelligence. Nonetheless, here are a few indicators that could prove useful:

- The depth and thoughtfulness of the answers

- The relevance and insight of the candidate's questions

- The level of mental alertness

- The candidate's grades and class standing

- Evidence of effective problem solving

Temperament

The sort of temperament a person has—sunny, gloomy, easygoing, demanding, etc.—doesn't always surface during an interview. Here are some additional things to look for:

•   How the candidate acts toward your receptionist and secretary

•   What sort of leisure activities the person prefers (social or solitary)

•   How the candidate reacts when you probe for more specific answers

•   Whether the candidate is pleasant during the interview

Creativity and Resourcefulness

Like intelligence, creativity and resourcefulness are elusive traits to measure, and too many people make the mistake of judging creativity on the basis of appearance. Obviously, it is illogical to assume that an individual with

135

an unconventional hairstyle or offbeat clothing is more "creative" than someone whose appearance and dress are more conventional.

If you correlate appearance with original thinking, you'll end up with employees whose creativity ends with their grooming. Here are some signs of creativity to look for:

- The amount of creative input in previous jobs

- Evidence in background that he or she enjoys solving problems

- The ability to simplify complicated problems

Confidence

Confidence is probably the most difficult trait to measure during a job interview, for two reasons: one, a candidate's nervousness may mask a sense of confidence; two, a candidate's intentional bravado may hide a *lack* of confidence. Here are some signs that can indicate the degree of self-confidence:

- General sense of self (how comfortable—or uncomfortable—the person seems to feel during the interview)

- Body language (particularly eye contact)

• Firmness of speaking voice

• How well the candidate is able to communicate accomplishments without overusing the word "I"

Motivation and Drive

Most candidates will go out of their way to *appear* dedicated to their work during the interview. The key here is to look beyond the motivation the person may be showing for this particular job and find out how motivated the candidate is in general.

Here's what to look for:

• Evidence of steady career progress

• Ambitions expressed during questioning

• How much the candidate has learned about your company

Keeping Your First Impression in Check

I appeared as "the real Robert Half" on the television show *To Tell the Truth*. The format, you may remember, was for three people, two of them impostors, to appear before a panel of "experts" and answer their questions. Members of the panel would then decide which of the three was telling the truth.

At the time I appeared on the show, it had been on the air nearly sixteen years. Even so, I found out from a producer of the show that the panel was wrong nearly two thirds of the time! (What makes this statistic even more surprising is that one of the three impostors in the show was usually an obvious giveaway, which means that the odds of selecting the right person were about 50–50.)

It's something you might keep in mind if you're tempted to rely heavily on your first impression.

Beware of the so-called halo effect. This term is used to describe what happens when you become so impressed with one aspect of a candidate's appearance, personality, background, or accomplishments that you ignore some serious faults.

You can become so dazzled by the thought of hiring a Phi Beta Kappa who graduated first in his or her class that you don't even notice how abrasive and sullen the candidate is, so it never occurs to you that hiring this candidate is almost certain to stir discontent throughout your department. You can become so impressed with a former All-American football star that you fail to notice his significant limitations. I recently heard of an executive who admitted that the main reason he had hired a candidate (whom he had to fire three months later) was that both had been naval officers aboard aircraft carriers.

The halo effect can arise when a candidate has been "presold" to you by someone whose opinion you respect, or when you're so desperate to fill a position that after a while *anybody* would look good.

Regardless of how it manifests itself, you must guard against it. My suggestion: allow for the halo effect in the overall impression you draw of the candidate, but do your best to keep this aspect of your impression in check.

Dealing with Your Prejudices

Many years ago a client requested an accountant. The client, who was in the jewelry business, had two requirements, neither of which had to do with ability. First, he told me, the person could not be fat. Why? Because "fat people steal." The second requirement was that the person could not live in Brooklyn. Why? Because "people in Brooklyn steal, too."

If the halo effect can blind you to a candidate's obvious faults, another common syndrome—prejudice—can produce the opposite effect: it can trigger irrational and self-defeating responses to "faults" that don't even exist.

Sad to say, I've had more irrational requests than I care to remember. I've had people tell me not to send them any left-handers because "left-handers are absentminded," and I've been asked to exclude candidates simply on the basis of what part of the country they come from. This is not to mention the illegal discriminatory requests that people are reluctant to discuss in public—biases having to do with the race, age, religion, or the physical appearance of a candidate. These days, personnel recruiters rarely get requests with illegal requirements, and when it happens we at Robert Half International offices turn down those requests. I'm sure most others do so as well.

In addition to the legal and moral implications of prejudices, they symbolize the irrationality that lies at the root of most poor hiring decisions. It's difficult for me to imagine anyone who operates under the influence of these biases being at all effective at hiring. People convinced that "women can't supervise men" won't give serious consideration to a woman and will often hire inferior male candidates. People convinced that employees over the age of fifty are too set in their ways will pass up a person with the specific experience and qualifications a job calls for, and hire a less-qualified younger person.

I've actively fought these prejudices over the past thirty-five years, and not just because I'm opposed to them on moral grounds. They represent bad business. I have yet to run into a successful company whose hiring policies were rooted in a stereotyped and prejudicial view of the world, and I have seen a number of *unsuccessful* companies in which this stereotyped and prejudicial view was rampant.

How to Tell When "Employed" Candidates Are Unemployed

Many of the candidates you interview who say they are still working are, for all intents and purposes, unemployed—that is, on notice from their present employers.

My own view of this issue is that it may not make any difference whether the candidate is employed or unemployed. The issue is whether the candidate can do the job. Even so, it may be useful to know if candidates who say they're employed are in fact unemployed.

You could, of course, ask candidates point-blank, "Were you fired?", but even if candidates are truthful when they say "no," you still have no way of knowing for sure if they were given the opportunity to resign before getting fired. You could ask the former employer, but many former employers will only confirm what was agreed upon at the time of termination.

All of which means you may have to use indirect means to get to the truth. You have to spot suspicious signals. Here are a few of them:

141

Blind-ad replies. Employed candidates who answer blind ads may well be on their way out. Otherwise, they would be more discreet.

Permission to contact at the office. Candidates who suggest that you leave messages at their office may have been given a secretary and office space as the last of the fringe benefits.

Résumés. According to one study, as many as 40 percent of those candidates whose résumés name their present employers or indicate they are "self-employed consultants" are actually unemployed.

Willingness to take a salary cut or make a lateral change. People who are secure in their current jobs will rarely consider a change unless it brings them more money or a very promising career route.

Willingness to travel a long distance to work. The greater the inconvenience the candidate is willing to accept, beyond what he or she has been accustomed to, the greater the likelihood that person is really unemployed.

Additional Clues

Here are some additional explanations for leaving a job that could indicate the person was fired.

- *"Personal reasons."* A catchall explanation that becomes all the more suspicious when the candidate refuses to elaborate.

• *"I was looking for a greater challenge."* Possibly, but this is a popular catchall phrase used by people who have been fired.

• *"Didn't see eye to eye with the employer."* Again, a possibility, but it's more likely that the employer initiated the action.

• *"I did so well the company didn't need me anymore."* Very few people have ever been fired because they did a good job. Companies usually find places for gems.

• *"Decided to go into business for myself."* Many employed people who decide to start their own business, particularly if that business is "consulting," have been fired.

There are any number of other reasons you should be suspicious of, but let me stress the point of this exercise. It is not to *eliminate* the candidate from consideration: it is to help you get a better understanding of the circumstances surrounding the termination so that you can factor these circumstances into your decision.

Even if a candidate is concealing the actual reasons for leaving, and even if the firing was merited, this doesn't

143

necessarily mean that the candidate is wrong for you. Remember, nearly everybody (80 percent, according to one study) has been fired at one time or another—and not necessarily for cause.

Remember, too, that being fired can often make for a *better* employee the next time around—assuming, that is, the person is someone who can learn from mistakes. Indeed, you can find out a lot about people simply by asking them to give you the reasons they were fired. People who blame the former employer for everything are not likely to have learned much from the experience, but those who admit to having made mistakes are showing maturity.

COMPARE YOUR INTERVIEWING ATTITUDES WITH THOSE OF PROFESSIONALS

If you've ever wondered how your own attitudes during interviews compare to those of personnel professionals, here's a chance to find out. Each of the questions below has been posed to personnel professionals in various surveys commissioned by Robert Half International. In column A, record your own answer. In column B, see if you can guess what proportion of survey respondents replied "yes" to the same question.

	A	B
	YOUR ANSWER (YES OR NO)	SURVEY RESPON- DENTS (YES)
1. Do you respond unfavorably to obesity?	_____	_____
2. Do you overlook specific experience if impressed with candidates' personality and intelligence?	_____	_____
3. Do you like candidates who are confident and assertive?	_____	_____
4. Are you more interested in personality than intelligence?	_____	_____
5. Do you pay attention to the way candidates dress?	_____	_____
6. Do you like candidates to look you in the eye?	_____	_____
7. Can you tell if candidates are exaggerating?	_____	_____
8. Do you like candidates who ask a lot of questions?	_____	_____
9. Do you respond favorably if candidates appear to need the job desperately?	_____	_____
10. Would you rather see candidates be overconfident than shy?	_____	_____
11. Do you prefer not to see candidates smoke?	_____	_____
12. Are you more interested in candidates as a "person" than in specific skills and background?	_____	_____
13. Would you seriously consider hiring those who were fired from their last job?	_____	_____
14. Do you hold being divorced against candidates?	_____	_____

	A	B
	YOUR ANSWER (YES OR NO)	SURVEY RESPONDENTS (YES)
15. Are you displeased if candidates know anything about the company?	——	——
16. Do you consider enthusiasm an important qualification?	——	——
17. Do you make a strong conclusion based on first impression?	——	——
18. Would you hold arriving late for an interview against candidates?	——	——
19. Do you let the physical attractiveness of candidates influence your decision?	——	——
20. Do you consider a comprehensive résumé important?	——	——
21. Do you like to see candidates appear to be ambitious?	——	——
22. Do you take into consideration the reputation of candidates' colleges?	——	——
23. Do you consider it important that candidates appear to be hard workers?	——	——

Answers
(Percentage of Respondents Answering "Yes")

1. 29   2. 62   3. 82   4. 20   5. 66   6. 69   7. 66   8. 77   9. 1   10. 68   11. 68   12. 18   13. 33   14. 1   15. 50   16. 84   17. 60   18. 36   19. 64   20. 97   21. 99   22. 77   23. 99

9 | *ON REFERENCE CHECKING*

*A bad reference is as hard to find
as a good employee.*

Getting genuinely useful reference information has never been easy, but it's even more difficult today, because so many companies are concerned about former employees who might sue because an "unfair" reference damaged their chances of being hired. Some companies are so wary of litigation, they won't even tell you that an employee has been terminated for such a serious offense as heavy drinking or theft.

Worse, I know one corporate president who becomes automatically suspicious when a candidate's current company gives too glowing a reference. His theory: the better the reference, the more anxious the company is to get rid of the employee.

Does this mean that reference checking is a waste of time? Hardly. Getting reliable reference information is vital, particularly when you consider recent studies that indicate that roughly one-third of all job applicants either doctor their résumés or misrepresent their accomplishments. Nearly 90 percent of the respondents in one of our Burke studies, in fact, felt it was important to *personally* check at least one reference before hiring anybody for an important position, and only 4 percent of the respondents disagreed strongly with the value of checking references.

True, obtaining reference information can be time-consuming and often frustrating. But valid reference information remains the most reliable way you have of verifying the impressions and authenticating the information you gained from the candidate's résumé and from the interview. So if the person you're hiring is going to be working for *you*, you should plan to do the reference checking yourself. Don't delegate the responsibility.

Whom to Approach for References

Let's examine whom it *doesn't* pay to approach.

References supplied by candidates—particularly personal references, such as friends, relatives, clergy, and co-workers—are not likely to be objective. The reason is obvious: no candidate is going to give you the name of anybody likely to be negative.

Not that you should ignore candidate-supplied references. The simple fact that a candidate is listing *only* personal references could be a trouble sign. When the reference list *doesn't* include the name of someone from a company with whom the candidate spent several years, it's possible something is being concealed. A candidate who lists *several* former bosses, on the other hand, is someone who probably *isn't* hiding anything.

Personnel departments are unlikely to know details about the candidate's day-to-day performance. And, since personnel people are usually very sensitive to the legal ramifications of issuing reference material, they are likely to be more reluctant to tell you anything about the candidate other than dates of employment and length of time in the company. Our Burke study found that top management was 134 percent more candid than personnel management when giving references over the phone, and 68 percent more candid when giving reference information in person. The message is clear: if you want useful reference information, aim as high in the company as you can.

Other Sources

Depending on the position, and so long as you get the candidate's permission, try to talk to some of his or her co-workers, clients, or customers who are familiar with the candidate.

Approaching friends of yours who know the candidate is a possibility, too, just so long as you don't automatically assume the information is completely valid. Our Burke study showed that top management gives candid references to friends only 67 percent of the time, which means that one out of every three references from a friend in top management could be less than candid. Personnel managers in the same situation admit they are candid only about 43 percent of the time, which means your friend in personnel is likely to be candid only about two out of five times.

A better strategy, perhaps, is to do some networking to get unbiased references. Ask the first reference you talk to in a company whom else you might contact at the same firm who might know something about the employee. Then, after you've talked with that person, get referrals to others at the same firm. The idea is to get information from as many people as possible who have no vested interest in protecting the candidate.

It's also a good practice to seek references from people who are specialists in the same field as the candidate. Such people are not only in a good position to evaluate the candidate's competence, they aren't as likely to be as reticent in sharing information as some others you may contact.

One final note: always verify education. Contact the schools and, with the candidate's permission, write for the transcript.

How to Obtain the Reference

There are three different ways to obtain references: by mail, in person, and over the phone.

The *least* productive way is by mail—for a variety of reasons. For one thing, as reluctant as former employers are to talk candidly about a candidate, they're twice as reluctant to put anything down in writing: it's too risky. According to our Burke study, only 45 percent of top management and 30 percent of personnel managers feel they can get candid information in writing, but only 28 percent of management and 24 percent of personnel are prepared to be candid in *giving* written references. (Most people, in other words, *expect* more than they're willing to give when it comes to references.)

Another problem with written references is time. When you request reference information by mail you have no way of knowing whether the person you're sending the request to is still with the company, or is out of town, or how quickly that person is likely to return the reference information to you—if at all. (I've known cases of requests for reference information taking weeks to get back to the original sender.) In the meantime, while you're waiting for the reference, you could lose a qualified candidate.

Clearly, the most direct way to obtain reference information, impractical as it might sometimes be, is in person.

Consider the advantages. When you talk to somebody face-to-face, you're better able to judge whether the person is genuinely enthusiastic about the candidate or is simply being diplomatic. As a general rule, people tend to be much more candid with you when you're sitting face-to-face with them rather than talking to them over the phone. Some 75 percent of top management surveyed in our

Burke study felt that people are likely to be candid when you approach them in person for a reference; 65 percent of personnel management felt the same way. The simple fact you're taking the time to see them in person is flattering to most people and is likely to make them more disposed to be candid.

(An interesting sidelight: while 72 percent of top management is prepared to give a candid reference in person and a roughly equal proportion [75 percent] say they *expect* a candid reference, only 43 percent of personnel managers are prepared to give a candid reference, compared to 65 percent who expect the candid reference.)

Most important, perhaps, if you can actually get to meet the candidate's former employer, you gain insight that would otherwise be denied you. You can observe firsthand the kind of person the former employer is—how demanding or easygoing a personality he or she has—and thus be in a much stronger position to evaluate how the individual might perform working for you, or whomever else in the company the person is going to work for. Here, in short, is why one of the most astute hirers I know would *never* hire a top-executive candidate without first meeting the former employer. "I'm as interested in the former employer as I am in the candidate," he explained. "I figure if the executive got along with a boss who is extremely difficult, that's a very strong point in the person's favor."

If a personal meeting cannot be arranged, the next best thing is to obtain the reference over the telephone. Here again you can expect resistance from the personnel department. Our survey showed that while 67 percent of top management was prepared to give a candid reference on the phone, only 29 percent of personnel were of the same mind. (And here again, we found an intriguing disparity among personnel executives—29 percent to 52 percent—between what they were willing to give and what they expected.) You can expect even less cooperation from references in the future, for more and more companies are establishing policies that forbid their employees to give employment information over the phone. That's why it's important that you approach the reference source in the proper manner, and that you follow some suggestions.

Asking the Right Questions

Try to begin any conversation designed to elicit reference information on a reasonably neutral note. One director of personnel I know no longer asks for "references." He uses the term "verification." Instead of saying, "I'm calling to find out what kind of person Mary Adams is," he'll say something like "We're thinking of hiring Mary Adams, and I'd like to verify a few facts with you." Once you've made the initial connection, assure the person you're talking to that whatever information is given you will be treated in the strictest confidence.

Your initial questions should deal with basics—the

candidate's title, length of time in the job, and general responsibilities. Your objective here is to verify résumé and application information and to get a handle on the candidate's level of responsibility.

Once you've gathered this purely factual information, try to draw some impressions from the person you're interviewing, making sure you phrase the questions tactfully.

Here are some of the questions you might consider asking:

- "What would you say are Mary's strengths?"

- "What would you say are her weaknesses?"

- "How would you compare her work to the work of others who had the same job?"

- "How much of a contribution do you think Mary made to your company or department while she worked for you?"

- "Is Mary the sort of person who gets bored with detail?"

- "Was there much on-the-job pressure?"

- "Was she absent from work frequently?"

- "Did she get to work on time?"

- "Was she honest?"

154

Regardless of which of these (or other) questions you ask, make sure you leave time for the most important question of all: namely, "Would you rehire Mary?" Pay attention to how long it takes the person to answer the question. If you sense hesitation, pursue the reason. "You seem a little reluctant," you might say. "Would you care to tell me why?"

Evaluating the Information

Two points are paramount when the time comes to evaluate the information.

First, reference information is, by its very nature, usually flattering to the candidate. This is particularly true of written references handed directly to you by the candidate. In fact, you can all but discount reference letters a candidate carries to the interview. Such letters are usually issued out of guilt or sympathy on the day of termination, and in many cases are written by the candidates themselves and signed by the supervisor. I've run into a few instances in which the letters were outright forgeries.

When you *do* run into an occasional negative report, however, don't jump to conclusions. I've known former employers who've come down hard on candidates simply because the employer was angry with the candidate for leaving. (Of course, if you come across the same kind of criticism from several former employers, that's another story.)

155

What to Do with the Information

Reference information should always be kept confidential, particularly if there are discrepancies between what you learn in your reference check and what the candidate has told you. If the discrepancies are very substantial, simply drop the candidate from consideration, and leave it at that.

Sometimes, though, you'll find some discrepancies concerning a candidate you're high on.

If the information you've obtained in your reference checking isn't overwhelmingly negative, give the person a chance to explain. (Don't reveal the source of the information.)

Be both tactful and firm. Don't hesitate to ask for names of people who might verify the candidate's version.

10 | *ON MAKING THE DECISION*

*The best person you interview
isn't necessarily the best person
for the job.*

Deciding which of the candidates you've interviewed will make the best employee is never easy. The more successful you have been at attracting quality candidates, and at weeding out those who are clearly unqualified, the tougher the final choice is likely to be.

The problem here is that the alternatives you have to choose among when you're making a hiring decision are not data you can feed into a computer. Even the "facts" you gather from the candidate's résumé and from the answers you get to questions during the interview are subject to interpretation. You have to decide how relevant this information is.

But, as with all business decisions, there is a logical approach to it. Then, too, if you have handled the preliminary aspects of the hiring process properly—if you've developed the correct criteria, recruited effectively, screened judiciously, and interviewed prudently—you've substantially reduced your chances of making a "wrong" decision.

You shouldn't compound the difficulty of the hiring decision by putting more pressure on yourself than is necessary. Keep in mind that no matter how much time you take to ponder, you can never be *absolutely* certain you've made the right choice.

Patterns to Avoid

Before I offer any specific advice on how to manage the decision-making aspect of hiring, let's look at some of these "traps" and how to either avoid them entirely or limit their adverse affect on your decision.

The "Cloning" Trap

It's human nature to be drawn to and to feel comfortable with people whose backgrounds and thinking are similar to ours. But to base hiring decisions on these same criteria—to fall victim to what is often called the "cloning" principle—is to shortchange yourself.

It seems clear that more than a few once-thriving companies are in deep trouble because their executive ranks are filled with people whose general background and philosophies are so similar that their ability to come up with creative solutions to problems has been seriously compromised. The most successful companies, by contrast, are notably diverse in the makeup of their top-management team.

More important, when you hire people who are little more than mirror images of you, the predictable result is a department or company strong in those areas in which you are strong, but weak in those areas in which you lack strength.

A much more intelligent approach to hiring is to follow the example of successful professional sports franchises, whose drafting strategies are based on *balance*: selecting each person for each position with the idea of how that person will affect the team.

"Fat People Steal, Don't They?"

I dealt briefly in chapter eight with the degree to which personal prejudices can interfere with the "reading" we make of candidates during the interview. The same principle is even more important to bear in mind when you're making the final choice.

True, it's impossible to remove *all* purely subjective considerations from the decision, but you should at least be aware of some of the most common prejudices that lead to poor hiring decisions.

- "Tall people are more self-assured than short people."

- "People who are overweight are lazy and lack discipline."

- "People who are physically attractive make better employees."

- "Older candidates are set in their ways and won't be comfortable taking orders from a younger supervisor."

- "Younger candidates are in too much of a hurry to get ahead."

- "Women are too emotional to handle pressure."

I could mention any number of other commonly held prejudices, but the point should be clear: to allow any of these prejudices to affect your decision is grossly unfair both to the candidate and to your company. Choosing good people is difficult enough as it is; add these prejudices to the mix and you increase the difficulty immeasurably.

"This Time It's Going to Be Different"

A few years after I went into business, a young man came to us looking for an office job and gave as one of his references a woman who turned out to be his mother. Because their last names were different, I didn't realize the woman was his mother until I called her, and rather than be rude, I decided to ask the mother for a reference anyway. "He'll stay out of trouble," the woman said, "as soon as he gets a good job."

In my first book, *The Robert Half Way to Get Hired in Today's Job Market*, I cautioned job seekers against trying to play upon the sympathies of the person interviewing them. My reasoning was that good jobs are almost never offered out of pity.

In retrospect, I should have amended that advice by pointing out that good jobs are almost never offered out of pity by people who hire *intelligently*. For there are some people who, no matter how many times they've been burned, believe that there is a magical quality about them—something that will transform a person with a consistent record of failure into a smashing success.

I don't mean to appear cold or callous here. Nor am I suggesting that altruism has no place in business, or that you shouldn't give people the benefit of the doubt.

But if there is one thing that behavioral scientists who study the business environment have discovered over the past few years, it is that the qualities that will most determine how successful a person is going to be in a new job are already there *before* that person is hired.

True, people can grow into jobs, and there are any number of factors that may account for a poor job performance in the past. But the principle here, as harsh as it may sound, is that the basic changes you can expect from people with a poor work record are minimal.

"The Candidate's Stronger Than I Am"

Candidates who appear unusually strong are often bypassed out of fear that they may pose a threat to the person doing the hiring. I can understand being concerned about your job, but I see no point at all in making a hiring decision based upon which candidate poses the least threat. If anything, hiring strong people can only enhance your own career, not only because good people will improve the efficiency of your department but because you will become known in your company as someone who knows how to choose winners. That's not a bad reputation to have.

Additional Keys to Successful Hiring

In addition to the principles I've alluded to in the traps just mentioned, here are some other points worth keeping in mind when you're making the hiring decision.

1. Focus on Accomplishments

The point bears repeating: the most reliable indication you have that a candidate is likely to work out well in the job is the candidate's track record. And a track record, remember, consists of *accomplishments*, not credentials.

Everything else being equal, look for the *proven* ability to do the job, or at the very least the *proven* ability to handle tasks that are similar to the job you're looking to fill.

2. Don't Try to Force the Fit

Your ultimate objective when making a hiring decision is to *fit the candidate to the job*—that is, to select the candidate whose strengths and weaknesses are best suited to the pluses and minuses of the job. With this principle in mind, it may become necessary on occasion to reject the "best" candidate in contention simply because that candidate is overqualified and is likely to quit the job as soon as something better comes along. Passing up excellent people isn't an easy thing to do, particularly in those situations in which the person appears extremely enthusiastic about the job, but there are only three situations in which I would deviate from this principle:

163

• The current position is one that can grow and keep pace with the candidate's aspirations to get ahead.

• The candidate is an "older" person who may not be interested in advancing a career.

• You're willing to get the most out of the candidate during the time he or she is with you, and you're willing to accept the likelihood that the employee will leave you in several years.

3. Picture the Candidate in the Job

Here's a simple exercise that can lend an added degree of objectivity to your decision. Try to imagine a typical day on the job—better still, a typical *difficult* day. Then, bearing in mind what you already know about the person, see if you can visualize the candidate actually doing each element of the job.

4. Put Yourself in the Candidate's Shoes

Once you've decided that a particular applicant is likely to perform well, try to view the job from the candidate's perspective. Keep in mind that most candidates want the job at the time they're applying, but may become disenchanted once they actually begin working. Here are the areas to focus on:

- **Career potential.** Does it meet the person's ambitions?
- **Work environment.** Is it likely to cause a problem for any reason?
- **Commuting time.** Could it be a problem, particularly in inclement weather?
- **Company style and philosophy.** Will the individual have any problems following company rules and procedures?

5. Give Special Consideration to Motivation

Within reason, the degree to which the candidate wants the job should always be a paramount consideration. This is not to suggest that you should hire the more motivated candidate over someone with more ability but less motivation. But when you have two candidates who are equal in most respects, give the edge to the candidate who wants the job more.

165

6. Limit the Number of Decision Makers

There's nothing wrong with getting input about specific candidates from other people in your company, but do your best to minimize the number of people involved in the actual hiring decision. The problem with involving too many people in the decision is that you almost invariably wind up with a compromise candidate—the candidate who is the least objectionable to most of the people involved in the decision.

7. Don't Settle

If you're not reasonably convinced that you're making the right choice, and you're not *desperately* in need of someone, don't settle. Consider alternatives: hiring somebody on a trial basis, or using temporaries until you've found a person in whom you have confidence.

8. If You Make a Mistake, Rectify It Quickly

A friend of mine who heads the human resources department of a "Fortune 500" company swears that, with rare exceptions, you can tell within a week after the candidate has begun work if you've made a good hiring choice.

"The trouble," he says, "is that many people would rather waste months on the candidate than throw in the towel early."

If you make a hiring mistake, rectify it fast—regardless of the cost, and regardless of your ego. Otherwise, you're not being fair to yourself or to the employee.

Using the H-I-R-E Form to Help the Decision

There are dozens of "systems" and rating forms that companies use to help bring a measure of objectivity to the hiring decision. Most of the ones I've seen, however, suffer from one of two shortcomings: they're either so complicated that you need an advanced degree in statistics to use them; or they're too fixed in their application: they're geared to one particular occupation.

The H-I-R-E form that appears on pages 168–169 has been tested by hundreds of companies and has proven itself to be an effective tool for managers who want to be as objective as possible when evaluating candidates. It's particularly useful when you need to choose among candidates who appear to be of the same ability.

Here's how the form works: you begin by assigning a relative value (based on how important that qualification is to the job) to each of five general areas of qualifications— Experience, Education, Intelligence, Appearance and Per-

167

ROBERT HALF®

Half's Interviewing Record and Evaluation

H-I-R-E℠

USE FOR NEW EMPLOYEES AND FOR PROMOTIONS FROM WITHIN

CANDIDATE'S NAME		POSITION	DATE	TIME
SALARY	ASKS $	EARNS $	WILL PROBABLY ACCEPT $	

QUALIFICATIONS	(1) VALUES Assign values to each qualification. Total must equal 10.		(2) RATINGS—Your rating of candidate on basis of 0 to 10 for each qualification	(3) EVALUATION Multiply all values in Col. (1) by ratings in Col. (2)	COMMENTS
EXPERIENCE		×		=	
EDUCATION		×		=	
INTELLIGENCE		×		=	
APPEARANCE & PERSONALITY		×		=	
OTHER		×		=	
TOTAL	**10**		TOTAL EVALUATION (Maximum 100) (4)		

ADJUSTED EVALUATION INDEX

Rate candidate's innate ability on basis of 1 to 5..............

Rate candidate's motivation on basis of 1 to 5..............

Total [insert in Column (3)] ——— + ——— (5)

ADJUSTED EVALUATION Multiply (5) × (4) maximum 1,000 (6)

This copyright system is the most effective method of comparing candidates for a position. The interviewer predetermines the relative importance of each qualification, and then rates each candidate accordingly. This results in an evaluation of how closely a candidate conforms to the qualifications. The interviewer then adjusts the evaluation based on his or her impression of the candidate's *innate ability* and *motivation*. (Sample filled in form on reverse side of this page.)

A nationwide Robert Half study revealed that the last person interviewed for a job is three times more likely to be hired than the first candidate. Yet, the last person is *not necessarily* the best.

Interviewers often have difficulty in accurately and fully recalling their objective impressions of earlier candidates which may make the last one *appear* superior to the others.

A skilled interviewer develops an intuitive sense that goes beyond strict adherence to predetermined qualifications. It is this depth of perception that causes instinctive recognition of a candidate's *innate ability* and *motivation*. Our exclusive H-I-R-E System enables the interviewer to give these important qualities the consideration they deserve.

INSTRUCTIONS

(1) Assign a Value to each qualification, based on your opinion of its relative importance to the job. The Values assigned are the same for all candidates interviewed for each position.

(2) Rate each candidate interviewed for each qualification on a basis of 1 to 10.

(3) To evaluate, multiply the Values you assigned (Col. 1) by your rating for each value (Col. 2).

(4) Add Column 3 for the Total Evaluation. (Maximum 100)

(5) Innate ability to do the job, and motivation are important factors. Rate the candidate on a basis of 1 to 5 for each attribute. Add the two together to produce the Adjusted Evaluation Index.

(6) The multiple of Total Evaluation times the Adjusted Evaluation Index results in the Adjusted Evaluation. (Maximum 1,000) This number is your basis for comparing all candidates interviewed for a position.

ROBERT HALF

Half's Interviewing Record and Evaluation

H-I-R-E.

USE FOR NEW EMPLOYEES AND FOR PROMOTIONS FROM WITHIN

CANDIDATE'S NAME: J SMITH   DATE 8/1   TIME 9 30
SALARY $45,000   POSITION CONTROLLER   EARNING $38,000   WILL PROBABLY ACCEPT $42,000

QUALIFICATIONS	(1) VALUES Assign values to each qualification. Total must equal 10		(2) RATINGS. Your rating of candidate on basis of 10 10 for each qualification	(3) EVALUATION Multiply all values in Col (1) by ratings in Col (2)	COMMENTS
EXPERIENCE	3	×	8	= 24	SEEMS LIKE A GOOD TROUBLE SHOOTER.
EDUCATION	2	×	9	= 18	
INTELLIGENCE	2	×	9	= 18	PERCEPTIVE.
APPEARANCE & PERSONALITY	2	×	7	= 14	TALKS FAST.
OTHER Cost Acctg.	1	×	10	= 10	MAY MAKE HASTY DECISIONS.
TOTAL	10			TOTAL EVALUATION (Maximum 100) 84	

ADJUSTED EVALUATION INDEX
Rate candidate's innate ability on basis of 1 to 5 5
Rate candidate's motivation on basis of 1 to 5 ..... + 4
Total (insert in Column (3).) 9

ADJUSTED EVALUATION Multiply (5) × (4) maximum 1,000 (6) 756 sonality, and any other qualifications you wish to consider. You can assign any value you want just so long as the total of all values is 10.

The next step is to rate the candidate on a scale of 1 to 10 in each of the same areas and multiply each of these ratings by the value in each category to get the evaluation. If you've given "experience" a 3 value and you've rated a candidate an 8 in this area, your evaluation in this area would be 24.

Once you've come up with an evaluation in each area, you're ready to compute the "adjusted evaluation index." Rate the candidate's innate ability from 1 to 5 and the candidate's motivation from 1 to 5 and add these two figures. Then multiply this sum by the total evaluation.

The procedure is complicated at first glance, but it's actually quite simple once you've done it a few times. What I like about this form is its flexibility. Unlike many rating systems, it can be used for any job: you simply adjust the values according to the job requirements. And it gives the interviewer the opportunity to consider in innate ability and motivation, which in my judgment often far outweigh other attributes. Plus one other important fact: in one of our studies we found that the first person interviewed has the least chance of getting the job offer (even though the first person interviewed may be the best one). The form will jog your memory so that in coming to a final decision you don't overlook the first ones interviewed.

Whether you ultimately offer the job to the candidate

who scored the highest is up to you. Now you have a reasonably objective basis for making the choice.

GIVE SERIOUS CONSIDERATION TO CANDIDATES WHO:

• Show proven capability to do the job

• Show achievements—not just past functions

• Demonstrate interest in the job

• Radiate enthusiasm

• Ask logical questions

• Prove how past experience and special knowledge will help your company

• Get to the interview on time

• Dress appropriately

• Have good manners and are not condescending

•Appear able to get along with co-workers

•Show loyalty to former employers

•Give the present employer adequate notice when resigning

•Offer you references to contact

BE WARY OF CANDIDATES WHO:

•Quit a job without adequate notice

•Accept salary terms and then try to up the offer

•Are pompous or rude to your receptionist or secretary

•Arrive late for more than one of a series of interviews

•Dress inappropriately or are poorly groomed

•Can't show achievements at former jobs

•Can't supply verifiable references

•Will have to travel very far to work—unless accustomed to doing it

•Will have to do substantial out-of-town travel and are unaccustomed to such travel

•Are overqualified (the exception: the older candidate)

•Reveal confidential information

• Are willing to violate a contract with a former employer

•Lack enthusiasm

•Lie about material factors

•Appear angry during the interview

•Didn't take the trouble to find out information about your company

•Seem to know very little about the company they worked for

•Take too long to think over an offer

•Talk badly about former employers

•Request that you match a counteroffer from their present employer

11 | ON LANDING THE CANDIDATE YOU WANT

You may not have a second chance to hire the best candidate.

It's one thing to select the candidate you'd like to hire, but it's something else again to *land* that candidate. In some cases, candidates simply receive better offers (often from their own firm), in which case there's little you can do about it other than to make the mistake of getting into an auction to outbid the counteroffer. Often, however, the candidate turns down the job because of something you—or your company—failed to do, and these are circumstances I want to focus on in this chapter.

Don't Delay the Offer

You should make the offer to the candidate as soon as you've made up your mind, and you should do it, preferably, by both phone *and* mail. If you have trouble reaching a candidate by phone, send the notification by a messenger service or one of the overnight couriers (if the person is out of town). Never assume, regardless of what the candidate has told you during the interview, that he or she is *waiting* for the offer from your firm, and will not accept another offer from another firm.

Time is crucial. I heard of a company recently that found it was losing 30 percent of the individuals who were to be hired simply because of its cumbersome approval process. If you are with such a company, you might consider offering the job on the contingency that the references pan out. It's better to make such an offer, in my view, than to keep the candidate in limbo for two or three weeks while the reference information is being gathered.

I'm not suggesting that you take any shortcuts or that you forgo reference checking for fear of losing a candidate, only that you bear in mind that the longer you delay in making the decision, the greater the likelihood that you'll lose somebody you want to hire.

Wooing the Reluctant Candidate

If everything has gone according to plan, the offer you make to the candidate should *clinch* the arrangement, and all you'll have to do is to work out the final details (starting date, salary and benefit package, etc.), which should generally be done in person.

There are times, as you know, when you'll run into a good candidate who hasn't fully made up his or her mind about the job. The strategy you take with such a candidate should be dictated by two factors: one, how much better that candidate is than other possibilities; two, the reasons behind the reluctance. If the reasons are relatively minor (a slight difference in salary, for instance, or some minor problems with how the job is structured), it's probably worth working things out.

But if either you or the candidate has to compromise a great deal in order to make the fit work, I would urge you to look elsewhere. I've discovered throughout my career that most of the reservations that candidates have about a job don't disappear once the candidate is hired but, if anything, tend to become bigger problems as time goes on. Candidates who aren't really sure, for instance, if they want to commute long distances or be away from their families for long periods of time are not good risks for jobs that require long commutes or extensive travel.

To be sure, it's worth sitting down with any candidate you'd like to hire to see if you can work out the differences. I see nothing wrong, either, when companies extend themselves to "romance" key candidates, just so long as they keep a reasonable rein on such efforts. Introducing the candidate to high-ranking officers in the company is often

177

ROBERT HALF ON HIRING

flattering to the prospective candidate, and if the job involves a transfer to another city, there's nothing wrong with inviting the candidate and his or her spouse to visit the city for a weekend for the purpose of getting a sense of how they might enjoy the city.

I want to caution you, however, about forcing the issue. Most of the outstanding candidates I've known who have quit, not long after being hired, had reservations about taking the job in the first place, but were persuaded by others (or persuaded themselves) to overlook these reservations. By doing too good a selling job to the candidate, you may win the candidate, temporarily, but the result will be a quick termination.

Giving the Candidate Time to Think Over the Offer

There is no generally accepted rule of thumb concerning how long you should give the applicant to think about a firm job offer. Mainly it will depend upon how badly you need that person or how much of a rush you are in to fill the position. I've been involved in situations in which candidates were given only a day to make up their minds, and I've been involved in situations in which the candidates had as much as a month or so to make a decision.

A month is excessive, but the point here is not so much

the amount of time you give candidates to say "yes" or "no" as that you set a specific time. They should also be informed that in the event you don't receive an answer by that date, you will resume your search. In the meantime, I would not give up the search entirely. The simple fact that the candidate needs more time indicates that there may be another offer pending, or that the person is having second thoughts about leaving the present job.

I'm not suggesting here that you generally continue to interview after you've made a firm offer, simply that you save all the applications, résumés, and notes made in connection with the search and that you gear yourself psychologically to proceed where you left off in the event that the answer is "no."

Confirming the Arrangements

As soon as the person is hired, you should set a specific starting date and salary and make sure the candidate is familiar with all company policies and procedures. If the person is currently holding a job, expect that the candidate will give adequate notice. Asking the individual to report immediately is unfair pressure on the person and is unfair to the candidate's current employer. If the candidate tells you that the employer "doesn't care," you might want to call the employer to verify. Months from now, you don't want that same employee leaving you without sufficient notice.

Don't Lose Touch

Once you've hired a candidate and agreed upon a starting date, keep in touch. The reason: you want to cement the relationship and counteract any second thoughts the person may be having since accepting the offer. Having the newly hired employee drop by after office hours to pick up some materials once or twice is a good way to keep the lines of communication open. You might schedule a lunch at some point between the day the offer was accepted and the starting date.

Legal Ramifications

The one thing you want to be careful of, above all, when you're hiring someone is that you make no commitment that could later come back to haunt you. If the job involves a contract, let your legal department or your lawyer handle it. Otherwise, say nothing and put nothing in writing that might be construed as a guarantee that you'll keep the employee for any specific length of time. If you write a letter of acceptance, keep the language neutral and non-committal.

180

12 | *ON FIRING*

The fear of firing causes firms to keep unsatisfactory employees who might do better elsewhere.

I had to fire many people during my business career, and I can tell you from personal experience that it never gets easier—at least it didn't for me. Even when there was ample reason (I once had to fire somebody we caught red-handed stealing from other employees), the very thought of having to tell an employee that we were letting him or her go was enough to give me a terrible headache.

I'm hardly alone, of course. Nobody I've ever met (or would choose to meet) finds it easy to fire, and I've known many people who agonize over firing far more than I ever did. What gets you through it, ultimately, is the knowledge that it's far better for everyone concerned—including the employee—to fire somebody who isn't measuring up than to keep people on your staff who aren't worth retaining. If it's any consolation, our studies have shown that except in rare instances, the terminated employee expected to be fired—or, at least, *should* have expected it if you've been a good manager. Only 22 percent of our Burke study respondents, for example, felt that firing came as a surprise.

But even if firing weren't as unpleasant a chore as it is, it would still pose a number of problems, and all the more so in today's legal climate. Time was when you could fire at will and not have to explain your reasons. Today, more and more terminated employees are suing their former employees on the basis of "wrongful dismissal," and are winning in enough instances so that companies are beginning to reexamine their hiring and firing policies.

So, apart from everything else you do in conjunction with hiring, it's important that your company have a *firing* policy. That policy should be in writing, should be detailed enough to cover any situation that could warrant dismissal, and should be part of the orientation kit received by each employee.

Don't worry about scaring off would-be employees with literature that clearly spells out your company's termination policies. Candidates who refuse to take the job because of these policies are probably not the employees you want.

It's one thing, however, to *have* a firing policy, and something else again to *implement* it. So here's some advice on how to make the best out of a bad situation and ease some of the pain for everybody concerned.

1. Give the Employee Warning

Except in very rare instances, a terminated employee should, as our surveys suggest, be expecting the decision. This expectation, however, assumes you've let the employee know all along where he or she stands. It is your responsibility as a manager to inform employees when they are not performing up to your expectations and, within reason, to give them a chance to rectify their shortcomings.

Do more than simply communicate your dissatisfaction. You have to make it very clear that the person's job is in jeopardy. (Some employees have an uncanny way of blocking out negative criticism, so that when they're told finally they're fired, they're shocked, even though they were given many warnings.)

One recommended approach is to establish a time limit for improvement. You tell the employee what you're expecting in the way of improvement and at what point you want to see this improvement. As one executive I know likes to put it, "If you know how to manage, you do so good a job of communicating what you're expecting, and when you're expecting it, you never have to fire an employee. The bad ones 'fire' themselves."

2. Be Sure of Your Decision

Although most people make the mistake of agonizing too long over the decision to fire, it's still worth stressing that firing should always be a last resort. Never fire out of anger, and always give the decision to fire as much thought as you give to the decision to hire.

The main thing to be sure of when you fire somebody, given the difficulties it creates, is that you've exhausted all other reasonable alternatives. Have you given the person enough time to learn the job? Would additional training improve performance? Have you done a good enough job of communicating what you expected of the individual? Have you given proper supervision? And if you're convinced that the employee is simply *wrong* for the job, is there another job in the company that the employee *could* handle?

I don't want to imply that you *not* fire somebody purely out of sympathy. Just be reasonably sure in your own mind that you've made the intelligent decision. The less certain you are, the more difficult everything else involved with firing becomes.

One more thing: keep your intention to fire to yourself. Firing is one topic it's next to impossible to keep out of the company grapevine. If you tell *anybody*, you can assume that the employee will find out.

3. Do It Yourself

If the employee works directly for you, firing is one managerial responsibility you should never delegate. It's not only unfair to the person to whom you delegate the chore, it's unfair to the employee, and it sets a bad example for others on your staff.

Common courtesy aside, there is still another reason for not delegating this chore: you must make sure that the firing is handled in a way that doesn't leave your company open to legal action.

4. Hold the Termination Session at an Appropriate Time and Place

Most personnel specialists feel that the best time to fire somebody (if there is such a thing as a "best" time) is late in the afternoon on a Friday.

But if you fire only on Fridays, and fire frequently, some employees will become so preoccupied on Fridays with whether they're going to be fired that they won't work efficiently. Friday may be preferable, but change the pattern now and then.

Whenever you choose to do the firing, make sure you set aside a block of uninterrupted time in a private place. If your office isn't private enough, find another location.

5. Be Prepared

Being prepared for firing an employee means having on hand whatever records, forms, or evaluations you may need if necessary to justify the decision. You should give the employee a memo detailing the amount of the profit and pension plan benefits accruing, along with any restrictions. It should include an explanation of the method of transferring medical and life insurance to the employee. And, most important, have the final check and the separation-payment check available to give to that employee.

6. Don't Drag It Out

Once you've called in the employee to be fired, deliver the bad news as soon as possible. Be tactful, of course, but don't beat around the bush with aimless small talk. The longer you delay in delivering the information, the tougher it becomes.

Here's a suggested approach: "Jim, it looks like things are just not working out, so I'm going to have to ask you to leave the company."

186

7. Don't Hold Out False Hope

The termination interview is not a counseling session and not the time or place to give the terminated employee a last chance to save the job. You've already made the decision. Your objective in the interview is to convey the bad news in the most tactful manner possible.

Sometimes, if you're dealing with an employee who you know is going to take the news badly, there's a temptation to lie about the reasons so that you can spare the employee's feelings. Resist the temptation. If you've decided, for whatever reason, that you don't ever want this person working for you again, it's a mistake (and unfair to the employee) to suggest that he or she might be rehired "when things pick up."

This isn't to say that you can't be honest and tactful at the same time. Simply focus on performance, and not the person. "I don't think this particular position was keyed to your strengths" is more tactful than "You weren't smart enough for this job."

Another technique that works well is to use the terminated employee's strength as a means of launching the criticism. "You're very good with people," you might say, "but unfortunately this is not a people-oriented job."

The principle, although not easy to follow, is to be honest but not brutal. If you go out of your way to be too tactful, you often do the terminated employees a disservice. By not revealing the reasons for the dismissal, you deprive them of the opportunity to learn from their mistakes.

8. Be Prepared for a Bad Reaction

You have no way of knowing exactly how the employee will receive the bad news, so be prepared for some severe reactions. I've had men and women alike break down and cry when I had to fire them. Others simply stared into space. And even though most people who get fired do anticipate it, the reality still comes as a shock.

I heard of one situation recently in which a man being fired simply refused to accept the news. "You can't fire me," he said. "I'll work here for nothing, if I have to." Such responses, of course, are rare, but they serve as a good lesson. If you lie about the true reasons ("We have to cut back on expenses"), you might have to deal with that lie later on.

Whatever happens, and as hard as it may be, remain professional. Be understanding and sympathetic, but don't encourage the employee to badmouth fellow workers, and don't make it seem as if you had nothing to do with the decision.

Probably the best thing you can do for an employee who has just been told that he or she has been fired is to give the employee some time to accept the news and then try to focus immediately and briefly on the employee's future. For example: "John, I hope you'll find a suitable position in a smaller, less structured company."

9. Don't Promise What You Can't Deliver

What you offer the employee in the way of support will depend primarily on your company's termination policy. Every company has its own ideas of what is and isn't fair in terms of separation pay, outplacement services, the amount of time the terminated employee can use the office, etc. My advice is to make every effort to be consistent with previous termination "fringes," or you'll only encourage others, who are fired in the future, to request the same consideration.

I've listed some of the various services that companies offer today to terminated employees. I'm not suggesting that you incorporate all of them into your termination policy—only that you think about them and develop your own criteria in each case.

• **Financial help.** Severance pay is usually in order, but just as important might be continuation of medical and life insurance benefits.

• **Office and secretarial services.** Some companies routinely provide office space and secretarial services for middle- and upper-level managers. But it can be awkward if the desk is close to former colleagues. If I were fired, I would not relish the idea of spending any more time than I had to in my old surroundings. I would rather deal with the secretarial and message services over the phone and have the correspondence sent to me by messenger. Such a practice makes sense for the employer as well.

• **Outplacement services.** A good idea, provided the employee is receptive and the service is reputable. Here again, when I put myself in the place of a person being fired, I would prefer a choice between an outplacement service or the equivalent in additional separation pay.

10. Be Sensitive to the Response of Other Employees

Whether or not other employees have a right to know why another employee was fired is not really the issue here. What is the issue is that a firing can erode morale and stir up paranoia if you're not sufficiently sensitive to the comments other employees will make to each other.

It isn't necessary to supply these employees with all the details, but try to answer some of the questions with a reasonable amount of candor. (Never discuss the reasons for the firing with other employees.) Keep in mind that the channels of communication between former and current employees usually remain open for quite some time.

11. Learn from Your Mistakes

If you have to fire a person, it usually means you made a hiring mistake. Trying to justify that decision may help soothe your ego, but it won't prevent you from making the same mistake again.

Ask yourself what led you to hire the person in the first place, and try to isolate where your decision went wrong. The more you learn from the mistakes you made the last time, the less likely it is you'll have to fire somebody else the next time. Keep in mind that our Burke study reveals that when candidates have to be terminated, management usually accepts the blame. The solution is to improve recruiting and hiring procedures.

How to Tell When an Employee Is Looking Around

Although everyone has the right to look for another job, it's not advisable to have somebody working for you who is looking somewhere else. In most cases, you should be able to tell when an employee is thinking of leaving, provided you're alert to some obvious clues. Here are some of these indications:

• Longer lunch hours and frequent absences (an indication that the candidate may be out on job interviews)

191

• More personal phone calls than usual (could be calls from potential employers)

• Sudden improvement in grooming and appearance (prepared for an interview)

• A neater desk (employee could be taking personal things home)

• A noticeable attitude change

• Change in vacation pattern

As for what you should do when you suspect an employee is looking around, I recommend three strategies:

First, don't beat around the bush. Ask the employee pointedly if he or she is looking elsewhere. Most people won't lie when you confront them directly, and those who do will somehow be obvious.

Second, try to retain a good employee. Arrange a meeting in order to find out what the problem is and what might be done to rectify it. In the event the employee has already received an offer, by all means resist the temptation to make a counteroffer. Counteroffers tend to encourage other employees to use the same tactic, and studies show convincingly that employees rarely last more than a year after accepting a counteroffer.

For those employees whom you would like to see leave, work out an *amicable* separation arrangement. It never does you or your company any good to have a disgruntled employee on your payroll. And it's always better to avoid, if possible, having a disgruntled ex-employee.

Legal Implications

Legal complications related to firing will arise primarily in situations where there is an employment contract or an implied contract because of alleged unjust dismissal. Otherwise, the main thing you need to concern yourself with when you're firing someone is that you don't leave yourself open to a discrimination suit.

The best way to avoid a suit is to follow the guidelines already spelled out, taking care to focus on *job performance* and not on personality. Give employees who are likely to be fired ample warnings, and be sure to make a record of these warnings for your file. I recently learned of a company that had to defend itself against a suit brought by a fired employee who had accumulated a massive record of absenteeism. But he was fired on the day he committed a relatively minor offense that had nothing to do with absenteeism. From the company's point of view, the offense was simply the straw that broke the camel's back, but because the company had never made a formal issue of his absenteeism, the employee felt that he was being discriminated against, and as a result won a small settlement. All of this could have been avoided had the company taken steps to warn the employee about the absenteeism. The possibility of a discrimination suit, however remote, is the best reason I can think of to be as honest as possible when you're discharging an employee.

It's also an excellent idea to think twice before you allow guilt to induce you to give a glowing reference to an undeserving employee who has been fired. It doesn't happen often, but occasionally a fired employee will take that reference and use it as evidence of an *unfair* termination.

13 | *CONCLUSION*

Time spent on hiring right is time well spent.

Successful hiring takes time and thought, and, like most skills, it also takes practice. On the other hand, the skills needed to make better hiring decisions do not necessarily require technical expertise. In the end, it's a matter of applying much of the same knowledge and instincts you apply to other business judgments.

Here is a summary of the principal points:

1. Make the commitment. Each hiring situation should be given top priority. The quality of the employees you eventually hire will invariably be a direct reflection of the time and energy you give to the selection. But make sure before you hire an outsider that you give consideration to competent employees within your company.

2. Familiarize yourself with the legal implications of hiring. The laws against discrimination in hiring are tough and getting tougher. It's easier than you may realize to break these laws. Make sure you and everyone else who participates in hiring are familiar with Equal Employment Opportunity laws and regulations, and be scrupulously careful that no aspect of your employment procedures discriminates on the basis of race, color, religion, national origin, age, sex, marital status, or handicap; and that all requirements are directly related to job performance.

3. Get a clear fix on the job. Take the time *before* you start your search to decide exactly what functions and responsibilities the job calls for, and make sure that the job, as you envision it, represents the most efficient use of personnel in your department or company. Once you've put together the description, key the qualifications to the functions, and don't restrict your possibilities by setting up too many mandatories. Double-check to make sure that there is a logical reason behind each "requirement" you set, and avoid the common mistake of giving too much importance to unimportant credentials.

4. Be realistic in your expectations. Your ultimate objective in hiring is not just to hire someone who *can* do a job but someone who will do an excellent job—*and* who isn't likely to become quickly disenchanted with the job or with your company. Take a hard look at the negatives of the job, and accept the possibility that in order to find a good person you will have to either lower your sights or take steps to make the job more attractive.

5. Choose your recruiting sources with care. The recruiting sources you choose should help you in two ways: one, reduce the amount of time you need to spend on the preliminary phases of hiring; two, assure you a sufficient supply of candidates who are genuine prospects for the job. And when using a recruiting service generally choose one that is a specialist familiar with the occupation, profession, or industry involved.

6. Monitor your screening procedures. Whatever method you use to screen candidates—whether you use a personnel recruiting service or the personnel department in your company—see to it *yourself* that qualified candidates are not being eliminated from consideration. Always ask to see a random sampling of rejected résumés so that you can make sure the sampling doesn't include applicants whom you would have selected for interviewing.

7. Become a better interviewer. For all its difficulties and limitations, the job interview is the most important tool in the hiring process, and you can't expect to hire intelligently unless you master some of the skills that underlie the successful use of interviewing. Make a plan for each interview you conduct (write down the questions you intend to ask), hold the interview in a private setting, and do your best to put the candidate at ease. Keep in mind that at the same time you're interviewing candidates, candidates are interviewing you and your company. Be professional and courteous, but don't be afraid to ask probing questions and don't hesitate to persist when the answers you receive are vague or ambiguous. Above all, *listen* with all of your powers of concentration and try to evaluate what you hear with an open mind.

8. Do the reference checking yourself. Try to speak directly (in person, if possible) to at least three people who can give you an accurate and candid opinion of each candidate you're seriously considering. Try to seek such information from some people whose names were *not* supplied you by the candidate but who were nonetheless in a position to evaluate the candidate's performance.

9. Do your best to be objective. Being *completely* objective when you're evaluating candidates and arriving at the final hiring decision is impossible. Accordingly, try to become more aware of—and to keep in check—any personal prejudices that could serve to eliminate qualified candidates from consideration in favor of candidates whose faults you overlook. Accept the validity of your impressions, but never forget that the most reliable indicator of future job performance is what the candidate has *already accomplished.*

10. Don't delay the decision. The hiring decision should never be rushed, but neither should you agonize so long over the decision that you lose good candidates. Accept the fact that there is no such thing as a "perfect" employee, and that you can never be *absolutely* sure that you're making the right choice. On the other hand, if you've defined the job properly, recruited wisely, and screened intelligently, your chances of making a "wrong" choice are minimal.

A systematic and intelligent hiring strategy will increase your success, the success of your company, and the success of the employees you have hired.

198

In the Appendix you will find a compilation of the data gathered by Burke Marketing Research expressly for this book. I urge you to read it thoroughly. You'll find it extremely revealing and highly useful.

On hiring: no one can be right all of the time, but it helps to be right most of the time.

APPENDIX

The following pages contain highlights of a hiring-attitude study that I conceived and developed especially for this book. It was conducted by Burke Marketing Research and consisted of a 10 percent sampling of personnel directors and top management of the "Fortune 1,000" corporations.

EXPECTED LEVEL OF CANDOR OF PERSON PROVIDING REFERENCES

	TOTAL (percent-age)	TOP MANAGE-MENT (percent-age)	PERSONNEL MANAGE-MENT (percent-age)
IN WRITING			
Very Candid	18.6	15.0	21.7
Somewhat Candid	18.6	30.0	8.7
Somewhat Cautious	37.2	35.0	39.1
Very Cautious	18.6	10.0	26.1
Don't Know	7.0	10.0	4.3
OVER THE PHONE			
Very Candid	25.6	25.0	26.1
Somewhat Candid	25.6	25.0	26.1
Somewhat Cautious	32.6	40.0	26.1
Very Cautious	14.0	10.0	17.4
Don't Know	2.3	–	4.3
IN PERSON			
Very Candid	34.9	35.0	34.8
Somewhat Candid	34.9	40.0	30.4
Somewhat Cautious	16.3	15.0	17.4
Very Cautious	4.7	–	8.7
Don't Know	9.3	10.0	8.7

PERSONAL LEVEL OF CANDOR IN *GIVING* REFERENCES ABOUT FORMER EMPLOYEES

	TOTAL (percentage)	TOP MANAGEMENT (percentage)	PERSONNEL MANAGEMENT (percentage)
IN WRITING			
Very Candid	7.7	11.1	4.8
Somewhat Candid	17.9	16.7	19.0
Somewhat Cautious	35.9	50.0	23.8
Very Cautious	20.5	–	38.1
Don't Know	17.9	22.2	14.3
OVER THE PHONE			
Very Candid	15.4	22.2	9.5
Somewhat Candid	30.8	44.4	19.0
Somewhat Cautious	23.1	16.7	28.6
Very Cautious	17.9	5.6	28.6
Don't Know	12.8	11.1	14.3
IN PERSON			
Very Candid	20.5	27.8	14.3
Somewhat Candid	35.9	44.4	28.6
Somewhat Cautious	15.4	11.1	19.0
Very Cautious	12.8	5.6	19.0
Don't Know	15.4	11.1	19.0

WHETHER A HIGHER LEVEL OF CANDOR IS EXPECTED IF PERSON *CONTACTED* IS A FRIEND

	TOTAL (percentage)	TOP MANAGEMENT (percentage)	PERSONNEL MANAGEMENT (percentage)
HIGHER LEVEL OF CANDOR *EXPECTED*			
Yes	67.4	60.0	73.9
No	27.9	30.0	26.1
Don't Know	4.7	10.0	—

WHETHER A HIGHER LEVEL OF CANDOR PREVAILS IF PERSON *REQUESTING* INFORMATION IS A FRIEND

	TOTAL (percentage)	TOP MANAGEMENT (percentage)	PERSONNEL MANAGEMENT (percentage)
HIGHER LEVEL OF CANDOR *GIVEN*			
Yes	53.8	66.7	42.9
No	33.3	22.2	42.9
Don't Know	12.8	11.1	14.3

EXTENT OF AGREEMENT WITH STATEMENTS
ABOUT GENERAL HIRING PRACTICES

	TOTAL (percent-age)	TOP MANAGE-MENT (percent-age)	PERSONNEL MANAGE-MENT (percent-age)
IMPORTANCE OF PERSONALLY CHECKING AT LEAST ONE REFERENCE BEFORE HIRING FOR AN IMPORTANT POSITION			
Agree Strongly	72.0	74.0	70.0
Agree Somewhat	15.0	12.0	18.0
Neither Agree nor Disagree	3.0	2.0	4.0
Disagree Somewhat	6.0	8.0	4.0
Disagree Strongly	4.0	4.0	4.0
MOST PEOPLE COMPANY HIRES PROVE TO BE EXCELLENT			
Agree Strongly	21.0	24.0	18.0
Agree Somewhat	60.0	54.0	66.0
Neither Agree nor Disagree	8.0	10.0	6.0

EXTENT OF AGREEMENT WITH STATEMENTS ABOUT GENERAL HIRING PRACTICES (cont.)

	TOTAL (percentage)	TOP MANAGEMENT (percentage)	PERSONNEL MANAGEMENT (percentage)
MOST PEOPLE COMPANY HIRES PROVE TO BE EXCELLENT			
Disagree Somewhat	9.0	10.0	8.0
Disagree Strongly	1.0	2.0	–
Don't Know	1.0	–	2.0
GOOD PRACTICE TO REHIRE COMPETENT EMPLOYEE WHO HAS LEFT UNDER FAVORABLE CONDITIONS			
Agree Strongly	38.0	30.0	46.0
Agree Somewhat	47.0	52.0	42.0
Neither Agree nor Disagree	3.0	6.0	–
Disagree Somewhat	10.0	10.0	10.0
Disagree Strongly	2.0	2.0	2.0
GOOD PRACTICE TO CREATE A JOB OR CHANGE JOB SPECIFICATIONS TO HIRE AN OUTSTANDING CANDIDATE			
Agree Strongly	10.0	14.0	6.0
Agree Somewhat	30.0	34.0	26.0

Neither Agree nor Disagree	14.0	12.0	16.0
Disagree Somewhat	26.0	28.0	24.0
Disagree Strongly	17.0	12.0	22.0
Don't Know	3.0	–	6.0

JOB REQUIREMENTS
USUALLY CHANGE AFTER
JOB SEARCH IS IN
PROGRESS

Agree Strongly	3.0	2.0	4.0
Agree Somewhat	29.0	22.0	36.0
Neither Agree nor Disagree	11.0	12.0	10.0
Disagree Somewhat	36.0	38.0	34.0
Disagree Strongly	20.0	26.0	14.0
Don't Know	1.0	–	2.0

GOOD PRACTICE TO HIRE
SOMEONE WHO IS
PERSONALLY
RECOMMENDED

Agree Strongly	4.0	4.0	4.0
Agree Somewhat	44.0	48.0	40.0
Neither Agree nor Disagree	25.0	26.0	24.0
Disagree Somewhat	19.0	16.0	22.0

EXTENT OF AGREEMENT WITH STATEMENTS
ABOUT GENERAL HIRING PRACTICES (cont.)

	TOTAL (percent-age)	TOP MANAGE-MENT (percent-age)	PERSONNEL MANAGE-MENT (percent-age)
GOOD PRACTICE TO HIRE SOMEONE WHO IS PERSONALLY RECOMMENDED			
Disagree Strongly	7.0	6.0	8.0
Don't Know	1.0	–	2.0
AVOIDANCE OF INTERRUPTIONS DURING A JOB INTERVIEW			
Agree Strongly	85.0	84.0	86.0
Agree Somewhat	10.0	12.0	8.0
Neither Agree nor Disagree	1.0	–	2.0
Disagree Somewhat	2.0	–	4.0
Disagree Strongly	–	–	–
Don't Know	2.0	4.0	–
MOST PEOPLE DO NOT FIRE AN EMPLOYEE WHEN IT SHOULD BE DONE			
Agree Strongly	22.0	22.0	22.0
Agree Somewhat	43.0	48.0	38.0
Neither Agree nor Disagree	9.0	6.0	12.0

Disagree Somewhat	19.0	16.0	22.0
Disagree Strongly	7.0	8.0	6.0

MOST PEOPLE FIRED
EXPECTED IT

Agree Strongly	13.0	8.0	18.0
Agree Somewhat	51.0	50.0	52.0
Neither Agree nor Disagree	12.0	18.0	6.0
Disagree Somewhat	18.0	18.0	18.0
Disagree Strongly	4.0	2.0	6.0
Don't Know	2.0	4.0	–

GOOD PRACTICE TO HIRE
REPLACEMENT BEFORE
FIRING EMPLOYEE

Agree Strongly	5.0	2.0	8.0
Agree Somewhat	11.0	18.0	4.0
Neither Agree nor Disagree	18.0	18.0	18.0
Disagree Somewhat	28.0	34.0	22.0
Disagree Strongly	36.0	24.0	48.0
Don't Know	2.0	4.0	–

INVESTIGATORY SERVICES
DO A GOOD JOB IN
VERIFYING INFORMATION
ON CANDIDATES

Agree Strongly	4.0	–	8.0
Agree Somewhat	36.0	34.0	38.0

EXTENT OF AGREEMENT WITH STATEMENTS ABOUT GENERAL HIRING PRACTICES (cont.)

	TOTAL (percentage)	TOP MANAGE- MENT (percentage)	PERSONNEL MANAGE- MENT (percentage)
INVESTIGATORY SERVICES DO A GOOD JOB IN VERIFYING INFORMATION ON CANDIDATES			
Neither Agree nor Disagree	26.0	38.0	14.0
Disagree Somewhat	13.0	12.0	14.0
Disagree Strongly	7.0	4.0	10.0
Don't Know	14.0	12.0	16.0
PSYCHOLOGICAL TESTING IS HELPFUL IN SELECTION OF CANDIDATES			
Agree Strongly	7.0	6.0	8.0
Agree Somewhat	32.0	40.0	24.0
Neither Agree nor Disagree	14.0	20.0	8.0
Disagree Somewhat	24.0	20.0	28.0
Disagree Strongly	17.0	6.0	28.0
Don't Know	6.0	8.0	4.0

INFORMATION ON RÉSUMÉS
AND APPLICATIONS
USUALLY ACCURATE

Agree Strongly	25.0	26.0	24.0
Agree Somewhat	59.0	58.0	60.0
Neither Agree nor Disagree	3.0	–	6.0
Disagree Somewhat	12.0	14.0	10.0
Disagree Strongly	1.0	2.0	–

ASKING FOR UNDESERVED
RAISE INCREASES
CHANCE OF GETTING
FIRED AT LATER DATE

Agree Strongly	2.0	4.0	–
Agree Somewhat	6.0	10.0	2.0
Neither Agree nor Disagree	14.0	16.0	12.0
Disagree Somewhat	33.0	34.0	32.0
Disagree Strongly	45.0	36.0	54.0

DO NOT HIRE A CANDIDATE
WHO WOULD NOT GIVE
ADEQUATE NOTICE BEFORE
QUITTING A JOB

Agree Strongly	34.0	36.0	32.0
Agree Somewhat	34.0	34.0	34.0
Neither Agree nor Disagree	14.0	18.0	10.0
Disagree Somewhat	14.0	8.0	20.0
Disagree Strongly	4.0	4.0	4.0

AMOUNT OF TIME REQUIRED TO FILL DIFFERENT POSI-TIONS

	TOTAL (percent-age)	TOP MANAGE-MENT (percent-age)	PERSONNEL MANAGE-MENT (percent-age)
AMOUNT OF TIME FOR UNDER-$25,000 SALARY CATEGORY			
Less Than 2 Weeks	6.0	2.0	10.0
2–4 Weeks	52.0	52.0	52.0
More Than 1 Month– Less Than 2 Months	28.0	24.0	32.0
More Than 2 Months– Less Than 4 Months	6.0	10.0	2.0
4–6 Months	1.0	–	2.0
6+ Months	–	–	–
Don't Know	7.0	12.0	2.0
AMOUNT OF TIME FOR $25,000-TO-$49,000 SALARY CATEGORY			
Less Than 2 Weeks	–	–	–
2–4 Weeks	18.0	10.0	26.0
More Than 1 Month– Less Than 2 Months	53.0	60.0	46.0
More Than 2 Months– Less Than 4 Months	22.0	22.0	22.0
4–6 Months	4.0	2.0	6.0

6+ Months	1.0	2.0	–
Don't Know	2.0	4.0	–

AMOUNT OF TIME FOR
$50,000-TO-$100,000
SALARY CATEGORY

Less Than 2 Weeks	–	–	–
2–4 Weeks	4.0	2.0	6.0
More Than 1 Month– Less Than 2 Months	25.0	22.0	28.0
More Than 2 Months– Less Than 4 Months	38.0	44.0	32.0
4–6 Months	17.0	18.0	16.0
6+ Months	7.0	4.0	10.0
Don't Know	9.0	10.0	8.0

AMOUNT OF TIME FOR
$100,000-AND-OVER SAL-
ARY CATEGORY

Less Than 2 Weeks	–	–	–
2–4 Weeks	3.0	–	6.0
More Than 1 Month– Less Than 2 Months	3.0	4.0	2.0
More Than 2 Months– Less Than 4 Months	33.0	34.0	32.0
4–6 Months	20.0	22.0	18.0
6+ Months	13.0	16.0	10.0
Don't Know	28.0	24.0	32.0

NUMBER OF PEOPLE WHO INTERVIEW CANDIDATES FOR DIFFERENT POSITIONS

	TOTAL (percentage)	TOP MANAGE-MENT (percentage)	PERSONNEL MANAGE-MENT (percentage)
NUMBER OF PEOPLE WHO INTERVIEW FOR UNDER-$25,000 SALARY CATEGORY			
1 Person	7.0	8.0	6.0
2–3 People	74.0	74.0	74.0
4–6 People	13.0	8.0	18.0
More Than 6 People	–	–	–
Don't Know	6.0	10.0	2.0
NUMBER OF PEOPLE WHO INTERVIEW FOR $25,000-TO-$49,000 SALARY CATEGORY			
1 Person	1.0	–	2.0
2–3 People	61.0	62.0	60.0
4–6 People	32.0	30.0	34.0
More Than 6 People	5.0	6.0	4.0
Don't Know	1.0	2.0	–

NUMBER OF PEOPLE WHO
INTERVIEW FOR $50,000-
TO-$100,000 SALARY
CATEGORY

1 Person	–	–	–
2–3 People	28.0	36.0	20.0
4–6 People	56.0	48.0	64.0
More Than 6 People	9.0	6.0	12.0
Don't Know	7.0	10.0	4.0

NUMBER OF PEOPLE WHO
INTERVIEW FOR $100,000-
AND-OVER SALARY
CATEGORY

1 Person	–	–	–
2–3 People	20.0	20.0	20.0
4–6 People	47.0	52.0	42.0
More Than 6 People	10.0	10.0	10.0
Don't Know	23.0	18.0	28.0

EXECUTIVE POSITION RECRUITING SOURCES USED FOR DIFFERENT SALARY LEVELS

	TOTAL (percentage)	TOP MANAGE-MENT (percentage)	PERSONNEL MANAGE-MENT (percentage)
SOURCES FOR POSITIONS IN UNDER-$50,000 SALARY CATEGORY			
Placing Newspaper Ads	94.0	94.0	94.0
Personal or Employee Recommendations	91.0	94.0	88.0
Recruiters and Agencies	84.0	86.0	82.0
Don't Know	3.0	2.0	4.0
SOURCES FOR POSITIONS IN $50,000-AND-OVER SALARY CATEGORY			
Recruiters and Agencies	91.0	92.0	90.0
Personal or Employee Recommendations	77.0	80.0	74.0
Placing Newspaper Ads	60.0	50.0	70.0
Don't Know	4.0	2.0	6.0

DETERMINING WHETHER CANDIDATE IS A HARD WORKER

	TOTAL (percentage)	TOP MANAGEMENT (percentage)	PERSONNEL MANAGEMENT (percentage)
WORK EXPERIENCE			
Prior Responsibilities at Job/Prior Accomplishments on Job	40.0	44.0	36.0
Work Experience/ Prior History	33.0	30.0	36.0
References	29.0	30.0	28.0
Past Performance	14.0	20.0	8.0
Length of Time on Job	5.0	6.0	4.0
Work Habits	4.0	4.0	4.0
Other	8.0	10.0	6.0
PERSONAL			
Interview Conduct/ Attitude/Energy Level	16.0	12.0	20.0
Hobbies/Outside Activities	5.0	–	10.0
Community Activity/ Involvement	1.0	–	2.0
Other	3.0	4.0	2.0

DETERMINING WHETHER CANDIDATE IS A HARD WORKER (cont.)

	TOTAL (percentage)	TOP MANAGEMENT (percentage)	PERSONNEL MANAGEMENT (percentage)
EDUCATION	15.0	12.0	18.0
Amount of Education/ If Completed or Continuing	7.0	4.0	10.0
Academics/Classes/ Grades/Academic Progression	7.0	8.0	6.0
How Education Was Funded/If Worked Through College	1.0	–	2.0
MISCELLANEOUS			
Psychological Evaluations/Testing	2.0	2.0	2.0
Quality of Résumé/ Cover Letter	1.0	–	2.0
Other	2.0	2.0	2.0
Don't Know/No Answer	3.0	2.0	4.0

AIDS IN DETECTING WHETHER OR NOT CANDIDATE
IS CAPABLE OF HANDLING THE JOB

	TOTAL (percentage)	TOP MANAGEMENT (percentage)	PERSONNEL MANAGEMENT (percentage)
WORK EXPERIENCE			
Success at Other Jobs/Prior Accomplishments/Responsibilities on Job	32.0	34.0	30.0
Job References	24.0	28.0	20.0
Work Experience	16.0	14.0	18.0
Skills/Technical Capabilities	16.0	16.0	16.0
Work Experience Compared to Job Requirements/How He or She Measures Up to Job Standards	16.0	14.0	18.0
Past Performance	13.0	20.0	6.0
Other	2.0	—	4.0
EDUCATION			
Education/How Far/If Continuing or Complete	22.0	18.0	26.0

AIDS IN DETECTING WHETHER OR NOT CANDIDATE IS CAPABLE OF HANDLING THE JOB (cont.)

	TOTAL (PERCENT- AGE)	TOP MANAGE- MENT (PERCENT- AGE)	PERSONNEL MANAGE- MENT (PERCENT- AGE)
EDUCATION			
Academics/Classes/ Grades/Academic Progression	4.0	4.0	4.0
Knowledge	2.0	4.0	–
Potential to Learn	1.0	–	2.0
PERSONAL	16.0	18.0	14.0
If He or She Fits the Job/Can Get Along with People in Job	6.0	10.0	2.0
Interview Conduct/ Attitude/Personal Characteristics	4.0	4.0	4.0
Self-Assurance	1.0	–	2.0
Other	6.0	4.0	8.0
MISCELLANEOUS			
Opinions of Other In- terviewers	4.0	2.0	6.0
Other	4.0	–	8.0
Don't Know/No Answer	4.0	–	8.0

HIRING PRACTICES IN THE PAST

	TOTAL (percent- age)	TOP MANAGE- MENT (percent- age)	PERSONNEL MANAGE- MENT (percent- age)
EVER HIRED SOMEONE WHO WROTE AN UNSOLICITED LETTER			
Yes	81.0	78.0	84.0
No	13.0	16.0	10.0
Don't Know	6.0	6.0	6.0
EVER HIRED SOMEONE WHO PLACED A "SITUATION WANTED" AD IN THE NEWS-PAPER			
Yes	11.0	6.0	16.0
No	86.0	92.0	80.0
Don't Know	3.0	2.0	4.0

MOST UNUSUAL THING EVER DONE AT AN INTERVIEW

	TOTAL (percentage)	TOP MANAGE-MENT (percentage)	PERSONNEL MANAGE-MENT (percentage)
EMOTIONS			
Anxiety/Nervousness	4.0	–	8.0
Crying	3.0	2.0	4.0
All Other Emotions Mentions	1.0	2.0	–
MISCELLANEOUS			
Left Early/Walked Out	7.0	6.0	8.0
All Other Miscel-laneous Mentions	23.0	20.0	26.0
Don't Know/No Answer	62.0	70.0	54.0

MOST DISTURBING EMPLOYEE BEHAVIOR

	TOTAL (percentage)	TOP MANAGEMENT (percentage)	PERSONNEL MANAGEMENT (percentage)
PERSONAL			
Lying/Dishonesty	14.0	16.0	12.0
Ego Problems/ Arrogance/ Overconfidence/ Aggressiveness	10.0	20.0	–
Lack of Dedication/ Commitment/Concern/Not a Team Player	6.0	4.0	8.0
Poor Attitude	5.0	2.0	8.0
Poor Listener	5.0	6.0	4.0
Not Get Along Well/ Not Communicate Well with Others	4.0	2.0	6.0
Whining/Complaining	4.0	2.0	6.0
Negative Attitude Toward Job/Company	3.0	–	6.0
Not Utilizing Full Potential	3.0	2.0	4.0
Laziness/No Motivation/No Enthusiasm	3.0	6.0	–

MOST DISTURBING EMPLOYEE BEHAVIOR (cont.)

	TOTAL (percentage)	TOP MANAGEMENT (percentage)	PERSONNEL MANAGEMENT (percentage)
PERSONAL			
Not Looking at Me/Not Looking Me in the Eye	3.0	2.0	4.0
Excessive Nervousness	2.0	2.0	2.0
Not Creative	2.0	4.0	–
Lack of Character/Integrity	2.0	2.0	2.0
POOR WORK HABITS			
Not Following Instructions/Not Respond to Instructions	5.0	8.0	2.0
Not Doing Job	4.0	2.0	6.0
Unproductivity/Not Accomplishing/Finishing Tasks/No Follow-Through	4.0	6.0	2.0
Goofing Off/Fooling Around/Personal Business on Work Time	4.0	2.0	6.0

Irresponsibility	4.0	4.0	4.0
Unreliability/Unpredictability/Inconsistencies	4.0	4.0	4.0
Not Following Company Policy/Procedure	3.0	2.0	4.0
Making Decisions Without Facts/Limited Information	2.0	2.0	2.0
Incompetence	2.0	4.0	–
ABSENTEEISM			
Absenteeism	8.0	4.0	12.0
Tardiness	4.0	4.0	4.0
Don't Know/No Answer	8.0	6.0	10.0

DAY OF THE WEEK MOST LIKELY TO FIRE AN EMPLOYEE

	TOTAL (percentage)	TOP MANAGEMENT (percentage)	PERSONNEL MANAGEMENT (percentage)
DAY OF THE WEEK			
Varies/No Usual Day	51.9	57.8	44.1
Friday	38.0	31.1	47.1
Wednesday	3.8	4.4	2.9
Monday	2.5	–	5.9
Tuesday	2.5	4.4	–
Don't Know	1.3	2.2	–

TIME OF DAY MOST LIKELY TO FIRE AN EMPLOYEE

	TOTAL (percentage)	TOP MANAGEMENT (percentage)	PERSONNEL MANAGEMENT (percentage)
TIME OF DAY			
Late Afternoon	39.2	35.6	44.1
Varies/No Usual Time	22.8	22.2	23.5
Early Morning	11.4	8.9	14.7
Midmorning	10.1	13.3	5.9
Early Afternoon	8.9	13.3	2.9
Early Evening	5.1	2.2	8.8
Noon	1.3	2.2	–
Don't Know	1.3	2.2	–

MOST FREQUENT MISTAKES MADE BY JOB CANDIDATES

	TOTAL (percent-age)	TOP MANAGE-MENT (percent-age)	PERSONNEL MANAGE-MENT (percent-age)
LACK OF PREPARATION			
Not Informed About Company	24.0	30.0	18.0
Unprepared for Interview	23.0	20.0	26.0
Don't Know What They Specifically Want to Do	6.0	8.0	4.0
Not Informed About Positions	2.0	2.0	2.0
Other	2.0	4.0	–
OVERPOWERING			
Too Pushy/Aggressive	7.0	10.0	4.0
Overstating Qualifications/Oversell	7.0	10.0	4.0
Talk Too Much	7.0	6.0	8.0
Too Well Rehearsed/Overpracticed/Unnatural	3.0	–	6.0

MOST FREQUENT MISTAKES MADE BY JOB CANDIDATES (cont.)

	TOTAL (percentage)	TOP MANAGE-MENT (percentage)	PERSONNEL MANAGE-MENT (percentage)
OVERPOWERING			
Egotistical/Overconfident	2.0	4.0	–
TIMID	15.0	14.0	16.0
Don't Sell Themselves/Don't Project Strengths/Accomplishments	8.0	6.0	10.0
Not Realizing Full Potential Accomplished in Past	2.0	2.0	2.0
Too Nervous/Overwhelmed by Situation	2.0	4.0	–
Too Negative/Talk About Bad Points Rather Than Good	1.0	–	2.0
Don't Talk Enough/Don't Ask Questions	1.0	–	2.0
No Enthusiasm/Too Passive	1.0	2.0	–

MISCELLANEOUS

Poor Personal Appearance/Not Properly Dressed	8.0	4.0	12.0
Trying to Hide Things/ Trying to Figure Out "Correct" Answer/ Lying/Not Candid	5.0	4.0	6.0
Criticism of Past Employer/Blaming Others for Past	5.0	–	10.0
Don't Answer Questions Properly/ Directly	5.0	4.0	6.0
Poor Communication Skills/Poor Grammar	4.0	6.0	2.0
Poor Listening Skills	4.0	–	8.0
Lack of Professionalism	3.0	4.0	2.0
No Eye Contact/Not Looking at Interviewer	3.0	2.0	4.0
Not Punctual	3.0	–	6.0
Smoking/Chewing Gum	3.0	2.0	4.0

MOST FREQUENT MISTAKES MADE BY JOB CANDIDATES (cont.)

	TOTAL (percentage)	TOP MANAGE-MENT (percentage)	PERSONNEL MANAGE-MENT (percentage)
MISCELLANEOUS			
Want a Job, Not a Career/Only Interested in Job, Not Company	2.0	2.0	2.0
Other	1.0	2.0	–
Don't Know/No Answer	5.0	2.0	8.0

MOST USEFUL INTERVIEWING TECHNIQUE

	TOTAL (percentage)	TOP MANAGE-MENT (percentage)	PERSONNEL MANAGE-MENT (percentage)
SPECIFIC QUESTIONS ASKED OF JOB CANDIDATES			
Personal Strengths and Weaknesses	9.0	8.0	10.0
Personal Background/ History	8.0	12.0	4.0
Accomplishments	7.0	4.0	10.0

Detailed Job History/ Complete Job Description	7.0	4.0	10.0
Details of Past Jobs' Strengths and Weaknesses	7.0	4.0	10.0
Reason Company Should Hire Candidate	5.0	4.0	6.0
Type of Preferences Previous Employer Would Give	4.0	2.0	6.0
Previous Performance Relevant to Position Sought	3.0	6.0	–
Educational Accomplishments	2.0	4.0	–
Former Supervisor's Strength	1.0	–	2.0
Short- and Long-Term Goals	1.0	–	2.0
Other	1.0	–	2.0
QUESTIONING TECHNIQUES			
Open-Ended Questions/Questions Without Yes-or-No Answers	17.0	12.0	22.0
Posing Hypothetical Questions	6.0	10.0	2.0

MOST USEFUL INTERVIEWING TECHNIQUE (cont.)

	TOTAL (percent- age)	TOP MANAGE- MENT (percent- age)	PERSONNEL MANAGE- MENT (percent- age)
QUESTIONING TECHNIQUES			
Open and Honest Technique	5.0	6.0	4.0
Probing Questions	3.0	6.0	–
Get Away from Specific Setup	2.0	–	4.0
Routine/Broad Questioning	1.0	2.0	–
Nondirect Questioning	1.0	–	2.0
Weave Questions into Conversation	1.0	–	2.0
MISCELLANEOUS			
Make Them Feel at Ease/Comfortable During Interview	8.0	6.0	10.0
Get Them to Talk About Job/Get Them to Ask Questions About Job	6.0	6.0	6.0
Ask References How That Person Could Improve	1.0	–	2.0
Honest Appraisal of Candidate	1.0	2.0	–
Other	6.0	8.0	4.0

WORST INTERVIEW EXPERIENCE (when respondent was looking for a job)

	TOTAL (percentage)	TOP MANAGE- MENT (percentage)	PERSONNEL MANAGE- MENT (percentage)
INTERVIEWER			
Rude Interviewer/ Lacked Sensitivity	8.0	6.0	10.0
Many People Asking Questions at Same Time/Interviewed by Many People	8.0	12.0	4.0
Lack of Knowledge of Interviewer	7.0	4.0	10.0
Lack of Attention/Interest by Interviewer/Indifferent	7.0	6.0	8.0
Unprepared Interviewer	4.0	4.0	4.0
Interviewer Did All the Talking/Never Had a Chance to Talk	2.0	2.0	2.0
EVALUATION			
Psychological Evaluation	3.0	4.0	2.0
Tests/Testing	3.0	–	6.0

WORST INTERVIEW EXPERIENCE (when respondent was looking for a job) (cont.)

	TOTAL (percentage)	TOP MANAGEMENT (percentage)	PERSONNEL MANAGEMENT (percentage)
MISCELLANEOUS EXPERIENCES			
Had to Wait/Was Kept Waiting a Long Time	9.0	10.0	8.0
Interruptions/Delays	4.0	2.0	6.0
Full-Day Interview	2.0	4.0	–
Other	18.0	10.0	26.0
None	21.0	26.0	16.0
Don't Know/No Answer	22.0	26.0	18.0

BEST INTERVIEW EXPERIENCE (when respondent was looking for a job)

	TOTAL (percentage)	TOP MANAGE-MENT (percentage)	PERSONNEL MANAGE-MENT (percentage)
INTERVIEWER AND CANDIDATE ATTRIBUTES			
Instant Rapport Between Us	7.0	10.0	4.0
Friendly Interviewer	6.0	6.0	6.0
Well-Prepared Interviewer	5.0	2.0	8.0
Informative/Explained Responsibilities/ What to Expect	5.0	6.0	4.0
Felt I Was Good Match for Position/What Company was Looking For	5.0	8.0	2.0
Interviewer's Attention/Interest	4.0	–	8.0
Felt Knowledgeable About Company and Job	3.0	2.0	4.0
Full Exchange of Conversation Between Us	2.0	2.0	2.0
All Other Interviewer and Candidate Attributes Mentions	2.0	–	4.0

BEST INTERVIEW EXPERIENCE (when respondent was looking for a job) (cont.)

	TOTAL (percent-age)	TOP MANAGE-MENT (percent-age)	PERSONNEL MANAGE-MENT (percent-age)
INTERVIEWING TECHNIQUES			
Quality Interview/Professional Handled Interview	9.0	4.0	14.0
Talking to Right People/Top Personnel in Company	6.0	4.0	8.0
Interview Went Smoothly	5.0	6.0	4.0
Felt Comfortable/Relaxed/Informal	5.0	4.0	6.0
On-Site Interview/ Tour of Company	3.0	6.0	–
All Other Interviewing-Technique Mentions	2.0	2.0	2.0
MISCELLANEOUS EXPERIENCES			
When I Got the Job/ When I Was Hired	17.0	20.0	14.0
Present Employer	4.0	4.0	4.0
Personable Boss	1.0	–	2.0
Other	4.0	6.0	2.0
Don't Know/No Answer	16.0	20.0	12.0

Index